D0708198

I am sure
I speak
for many
others

I am sure I speak for many others

COLIN SHINDLER

1 3 5 7 9 10 8 6 4 2

BBC Books, an imprint of Ebury Publishing
20 Vauxhall Bridge Road,
London SW1V 2SA

BBC Books is part of the Penguin Random House group of
companies whose addresses can be found at global.
penguinrandomhouse.com

Penguin
Random House
UK

First published by BBC Books in 2017

www.penguin.co.uk

A CIP catalogue record for this book is available from the British
Library

ISBN 9781785942532

Typeset in India by Integra Software Services Pvt. Ltd, Pondicherry

Printed and bound in Great Britain by Clays Ltd, St Ives PLC

Penguin Random House is committed to a sustainable future for our
business, our readers and our planet. This book is made from Forest
Stewardship Council® certified paper.

CONTENTS

THE BBC WRITTEN ARCHIVE

For nearly a hundred years there has been a broadcasting organisation called the BBC. And for nearly a hundred years the people who watch and listen to its programmes have been writing letters to complain about them and to praise them. These letters are a barometer of our changing social attitudes.

In a corner of the grounds of Caversham Park, a few miles outside Reading, sits a small and undistinguished white 1930s bungalow. If it weren't for the BBC sign outside you would pass down the suburban street it faces without a second glance. As you enter the building you are transported back in time, to a GP's practice in a county town, or your grandmother's hall. But this is all an illusion. For once the door is closed, this modest bungalow seemingly goes on forever. Behind the unassuming frontage and entrance hall lie numerous extensions and new buildings; each room is filled to the brim with the production notes, requests and forms that are a fundamental part of programme making. If, for example, you want to know how many extras were asked for by Ian Macnaughton, the producer of *Monty Python's Flying Circus,* for the filming of the Upper Class Twit of the Year sketch you will be able to find the answer. Much more interesting, however, are the files of letters dating back to the start of the BBC in 1922. These are the true glory of the BBC Written Archive.

The files labelled 'Reports on Programme Correspondence' contain monthly reports. The file for May 1958, for example, reveals that during that month the BBC received 12,944 letters. The Telephone Correspondence file for the same month shows they also received a further 181 phone calls. Perhaps not surprisingly, the BBC has not kept all 12,944 letters. Instead it was the job of Kathleen Haacke for over twenty years, from the late 1940s right through to the 1960s, and later that decade the delightfully named Betty Kitcat, to summarise the correspondence received and to extract sections of particular interest. The selections that Kathleen, Betty and their successors made are the first step in our journey into the minds of the British public throughout the second half of the twentieth century.

To an extent the letters have been pre-selected. Not every file from every production was sent to Caversham. The decision to destroy the files instead of sending them to Caversham might have been made by an overworked production secretary or a producer who did not think his or her programme would be the subject of historical study decades later. Not every production file which was eventually sent to Caversham has been retained by the Archive, mostly, I am assured, for reasons of space but since none of the programmes I produced for the BBC over a period of twenty years are there I am inclined to attribute the decision to pure caprice (or malice).

There is an overwhelming preponderance of letters from the 1960s, the decade in which Hugh Carleton Greene was the Director General and the decade in which the BBC lost its stuffy 1950s 'Auntie' image and opened itself up to stories and ideas which reflected the social turmoil of the time. Greene had been a journalist in Berlin during the inter-war years and had been much influenced by the cabaret culture of Weimar Germany. He had also seen at first hand the impact of the dead hand of government on cultural expression during the Nazi years before the war. It was Greene who made it possible for men like Sydney Newman, the innovative Head of Drama who brought working class drama to the screen, and Huw Wheldon, who edited the pioneering arts strand *Monitor,* to hire the people who created the BBC's reputation for artistic excellence.

Nobody disputed the distinction of series like Kenneth Clark's *Civilisation*, Alistair Cooke's *America*, David Attenborough's *Life on Earth* or Jacob Bronowski's *The Ascent of Man*. However, many of the groundbreaking productions of the BBC in the

1960s were not received with unanimous acclaim despite their current iconic status. The comedy series *Steptoe and Son* and *Till Death Us Do Part* were thought to be vulgar and blasphemous. *Z Cars* was a police series whose gritty portrayals of life on the streets of Kirkby, a suburb of Liverpool (or Newtown as it was called in the programme), shocked audiences that had been happy to believe that P.C. George Dixon could keep the London borough of Dock Green free of crime with a clip round the ear of a teenage delinquent. *The Wednesday Play* (or *Play for Today* as it became) included major works by Dennis Potter, Ken Loach and Tony Garnett. *Cathy Come Home* and *Up the Junction* are the most famous examples of this strand and their depictions of homelessness and illegal back street abortion in Clapham horrified and outraged many.

As Greene threw open the windows and tried to let in the outside air, many thousands of licence fee payers believed that he had merely let in the stinking and polluted air rising from the sewers, and the result of their protests was the start of the Clean Up TV Campaign, led by Mary Whitehouse, who regarded Hugh Greene as Public Enemy Number One. As we can see from the chapter on Radio Swearing, certain sections of the British public had long made its objections known to what it regarded as blasphemous and obscene, but it was in the 1960s that the letters poured into the BBC in a veritable torrent because these new programmes were part of a deliberate effort on the part of the Corporation under Greene's directorship to tackle controversial subjects like sex, religion, the monarchy and Parliament, which the BBC had traditionally eschewed. It was believed by the outraged correspondents that in transmitting plays with a title like *The Year of the Sex Olympics,* or letting David Frost and Ned Sherrin satirise the Queen, Harold Macmillan and Alec Douglas-Home, or possibly worst of all, letting Kenneth Tynan say the word 'fuck' on a late-night television discussion about censorship, the BBC was betraying its traditional role in British life.

There was a reason why the BBC was the nation's favourite 'Auntie'. The BBC had had 'a good war'. The voices of Alvar Lidell and John Snagge reading the news or Richard Dimbleby and Wynford Vaughan-Thomas reporting from the front line had been extremely reassuring to people who had been facing the real possibility of invasion, defeat and occupation by a barbaric foe. Just as the women who had succeeded triumphantly in the workplace during the war were escorted back to domestic routine when the men came home, so the BBC in the 1950s seemed to retreat with a sigh of relief to the safety of *Workers' Playtime, Music While You Work, Animal, Vegetable, Mineral?* and *What's My Line?*

When Greene, Wheldon and Newman abandoned this safety net and deliberately sought new, difficult and challenging areas of programme-making, many people were confronted by a stream of images and ideas which they found unpleasant if not frightening. Much was made in the post-war years of the atmosphere in which young children could grow up and prosper, free from the Depression, war and austerity that had blighted the early years of their parents in the 1930s and 1940s. The BBC had a part to play in this idea, it was believed, but by promoting Alf Garnett, Albert Steptoe and David Frost, Hugh Greene's BBC had seemingly abandoned the ethos of middle-class values and deference to traditional authority which had been the hallmark of its behaviour since 1922. It had not opened the door to a new cultural freedom: instead, it had stimulated and encouraged a collapse of moral values.

This was the kind of thinking that persuaded the letter writers of the 1960s to implore BBC executives to cancel shows like *That Was the Week That Was* and *Till Death Us Do Part*. In writing such letters, they believed that it was within the power of the BBC to restore Britain to the place it had held as a great power before 1945.

There are many letters in this collection that will make readers of today smile if not laugh out loud, though beneath the smile is a more serious intention.

They are fascinating historical documents, and the letters are reproduced exactly as written including the spelling mistakes. Some of the longer letters have been trimmed of their repetitions but all the words are those of the original authors. Annotated comments in square brackets or in italics are mine.

The traditional BBC response to a letter addressed to the Director General was usually a printed postcard thanking the author for the views expressed, of which note would be duly (not) taken. It didn't do much for the frustrated author who was confronted with the stark realisation of the waste of a threepenny stamp. On the other hand, some letters addressed to specific individuals by name did produce a personal response. In the files there are to be found many well written and carefully worded responses that did more than simply acknowledge the original letter.

There are copies of a number of letters written by Huw Wheldon which elicit nothing but the greatest admiration. He does understand why viewers are getting so worked up by bad taste, swearing and, as they now say, 'scenes of a sexual nature', which in 2017 are as nothing in a television climate that includes a naked dating series at 10 p.m. on Channel 4. Wheldon tries sincerely and with passion to explain why artists need to venture down avenues of human behaviour which make some audiences uncomfortable. He begs their forgiveness and appreciates the anger they feel but he believes that writers and programme-makers must be allowed to explore their own originality and creativity, which might also mean the inclusion of words and ideas that some people will find offensive. It is a thoroughly admirable and eloquent defence of artistic freedom but it has not been included herein because the book was always intended to showcase only the views of the general viewing public.

An attempt has been made to preserve the anonymity of the writers except in certain circumstances when the author is a public figure: for example, Clement Attlee, shortly to become the Prime Minister, Geoffrey Fisher, Archbishop of Canterbury and, inevitably, Mrs Mary Whitehouse. Her rather gentle chiding of the BBC in 1961 in neat handwriting on a small piece of lavender-coloured stationery, stands in marked contrast to her much more strident communications and demands later in the decade. It is of course appreciated that these letters were not written with the intention of ultimate publication so the addresses from which they originated have been shortened to make identification impossible.

After considerable research it might be possible to identify who the Honorary Secretary of the Skegness Hoteliers Association was when the gentleman who held that distinguished office wrote in to protest about the BBC's outrageous implication that the air in Skegness was not as bracing as the inhabitants of that Lincolnshire coastal town had always maintained. It would, however, be a rather pointless exercise since he was only doing the job he had been appointed to carry out.

I am Sure I Speak for Many Others ... is the story of the people's BBC, because from these letters we can learn a great deal about Britain and the British people in the years since the end of World War II. Who are the people who write these letters? Why are they so unbelievably upset about things that appear to us now to be astonishingly trivial? Why can't a lot of them, who appear to have enjoyed the benefit of a good education, nevertheless reveal themselves as unable to spell properly? (Maybe texting, internet trolling and comprehensive school education aren't the only reasons for the current blight of appalling spelling.) More importantly, what do those letters and the programmes that inspired them tell us about how life used to be in Great Britain? The answer is that, taken as a whole, the letters contained in this book tell us exactly how we have become the nation we now are.

THE DUTY OFFICER'S REPORT

In the days before radio phone-ins, emails, blogs and internet trolls, the general public had two principal ways of making the BBC aware of their observations on its programmes. One way, of course, was to write a letter or preferably, as the BBC would always politely remind its viewers and listeners, 'a postcard'. This was intended to keep the complaints brief but, as the following pages indicate, nothing really replaced a good loud moan on the Basildon Bond.

The other way was to telephone BBC Television Centre in London on 743 8000, which got you through to the main switchboard. Out of hours, i.e. during the course of the evening when the programmes were actually broadcast, the telephone was invariably answered by an elderly commissionaire in uniform with a peaked cap, armed with a pencil and a pad of lined paper. Painstakingly, he wrote down the litany of complaints from the licence fee payers who were invariably irritated that they could not speak directly to the person responsible for their irritation.

The Duty Officers' logs were then typed up and circulated to the relevant department the following day. There was the occasional paean of praise but, like the letters, they were far outweighed by the complaints. However, it was recognised by the BBC that these protests were a useful way of keeping track of exactly what the licence payers felt strongly about and, again like the letters, they provide a helpful guide to contemporary reaction.

If we take a typical evening, say Saturday 18 January 1975, we get a fairly typical cross-section of telephone calls. Bear in mind this was the BBC at its strongest. The lineup of programmes included such ratings stalwarts as *Doctor Who, Jim'll Fix It, All Creatures*

Great and Small, Kojak, The Generation Game, The Two Ronnies, then *Match of the Day* and *Parkinson*. It might have terrified ITV, who could never find the smallest dent in that lineup, but it didn't impress some of the viewers. The BBC commissionaire licked his pencil stub and began to transcribe the phone calls ...

LULU
A lady: What have you done to Lulu? She has no tone, and she looks terrible.

WEATHER
Tell Barbara Edwards she's talking a load of rubbish. It's bucketing down in Epsom and has been all day, and she said all rain had finished and moved her little black dots off the map.

DOCTOR WHO
Anon. man: Thought that the new series of this programme was absolutely pathetic, even for children of 43. There were holes in the plot and it was like watching a leaky sieve.

NEWS
Anon. man: Screamed down the telephone that he wished to speak to someone in the News department because, he claimed, during the course of the bulletin the word 'project' had been pronounced two different ways, i.e. 'project' and 'prowject' and he wished to complain. He was told that his complaint would be noted by the D[uty] O[fficer] and passed to News but he refused to leave his name, went on shouting very loudly, said I had obviously never been to school, was extremely unintelligent, and could go and drown myself – at which point I hung up.

All this, the DO must have been thinking, for £38.53 a week less tax deducted at source. And now for something completely similar ... *I Am Sure I Speak for Many Others: Unpublished Letters to the BBC.*

STAR LETTER

This is possibly the most brilliant suggestion for a new and original BBC radio series ever submitted by a listener ...

New Malden, Surrey
15 January 1946

To: Messrs. The British Broadcasting Corporation, London

Dear Sirs,

That you do your utmost to please all 'listeners' is, I am sure, to be appreciated.

There is, however, one section of the public for whom, to the best of my knowledge, you have never catered.

A great opportunity will shortly present itself.

Why not give us an hour of Chess? – a game between Dr. Tartakowa, this year's Hastings Champion and the winner of the International Tournament now in progress in London.

Thousands of Chess enthusiasts would be ready with boards and record pads.

Something new – Something Great!

Yours truly

N. R.

No record of a reply to this innovative idea is to be found in the BBC Archive ....

CHAPTER ONE

CHILDREN'S PROGRAMMES

You would have to have been born before 1945 to have grown up in a Britain when children's programmes meant those broadcast on the radio. Baby boomers might have had an early exposure to the comforting voice of that supreme storyteller Daphne Oxenford on *Listen with Mother* saying, 'Are you sitting comfortably? Then I'll begin,' but, for most of us, children's programmes meant what was on television.

In the 1950s, after graduating from *Muffin the Mule*, children found that their programmes quickly assumed a familiar schedule. Freda Lingstrom, who had devised *Listen with Mother,* became Head of Children's Television and predictably converted her radio ratings smash into *Watch with Mother*, the umbrella title under which very British middle-class programmes prospered. It was *The Woodentops* on Mondays, *Andy Pandy* on Tuesdays, *The Flower Pot Men* on Wednesdays, *Rag, Tag and Bobtail* on Thursdays and whatever it was on Fridays was so unmemorable I've forgotten it. I think it might have been something called *Picture Book*. These programmes only lasted ten or fifteen minutes and they contained a lot of puppets with visible strings. Nevertheless, so far, so comforting and undoubtedly so uncontroversial.

Andy Pandy, The Flower Pot Men and *The Woodentops* were created by Lingstrom herself, aided by the writer-narrator Maria

Bird, with whom she shared a home for four decades. In fact, the output was dominated by women: of the seven producers originally allocated to the department, four were female. Perhaps understandably, then, there was a significant maternal comfort to these BBC programmes, in marked contrast to the American 'rubbish' which dominated the ITV children's schedule and with which Lingstrom refused to sully the BBC's reputation.

Unfortunately, children preferred American cartoons like *Huckleberry Hound* and *Popeye,* to say nothing of *Davy Crockett* and the homemade *Robin Hood.* As BBC audiences switched wholesale to the newly formed ITV, the Corporation was forced to compete and soon the American series of westerns, *The Cisco Kid, The Lone Ranger, Hopalong Cassidy* and *Bronco* came to dominate the schedules of BBC children's television, much to the disgust of the now departed Lingstrom. There were still plenty of extremely good adaptations of classic books on the BBC – *The Silver Sword, The Children of the New Forest* and so on but there was a realisation by the Children's department that they needed to innovate.

Like much else in this book it becomes apparent that as children's programming began to expand its horizons in the 1960s, it attracted instant opprobrium. *Doctor Who*, which started in 1963, was an immediate hit with children but an object of terror for parents. Teenagers would happily spend many hours of a school day chanting 'Exterminate, exterminate!' with an arm stretched out in front to imitate a Dalek, but for pre-teen children whose parents thought they were getting a harmless science fiction adventure it quickly became an argumentative battleground. What had been regarded as the staple children's programmes on the BBC – *Billy Bunter of Greyfriars School, Captain Pugwash, Pinky and Perky, The Sooty Show* and perhaps an adaptation of *Ballet Shoes* – were no longer enough. They were safe, they were entertaining, certainly, but they weren't edgy. *Doctor Who*, for all its 99p special effects, captured children's imaginations – which, the BBC could justifiably point out in its defence, was what its children's programmes were supposed to do.

Alongside its drama there began in 1958 a programme that was still going strong sixty years later. It was a shame that a British pacifist organisation seemed to get hold of the wrong end of the stick ....

Peace Pledge Union, Endsleigh St., London WC1

22 July 1960

To: The Director General, British Broadcasting Corporation, Broadcasting House W1

Dear Director General,

We have seen with much concern that the BBC are putting on a series of six programmes on television under the title 'Blue Peter'. It would seem that the programme is a recruiting effort primarily designed to persuade young lads to enter the RAF. Like other recruiting methods it will doubtless appeal to youngsters and their love of adventure by showing all the attractive side of life in the RAF. May I ask whether it will also show the other side and make them aware of what the consequences might be of manning a fighter aircraft and still more a V-bomber carrying the H-bomb?

However much the programme may disguise the essential facts, it remains true that the end product of training in the RAF is violence. To accustom them to the worst form of warfare and even to make the H-bomb a symbol of adventurous service, is to do the gravest disservice to our young people.

Will the BBC give facilities for the pacifist appeal to be put to our young people and present a similar series which would appeal to their sense of adventure in ways which are beyond doubt beneficial to humanity and of positive service to the community?

Yours sincerely,

M.S.

Band of Hope Union, London SW1

3 November 1964

To: Sir Hugh Greene, K.C.M.G. O.B.E., Director General, B.B.C., Broadcasting House London W1

Dear Sir,

I am instructed by my chairman, Sir Cyril Black, M.P. to make urgent representations to you in the following matter.

On Thursday evening last in the 'Blue Peter' programme a recipe for Ginger Beer was given, and the children were invited to write for a copy of it. We understand 9,000 children applied for this recipe by first post Monday morning.

We have sought expert opinion on this particular recipe, and are satisfied that it is a brewing process which produces alcohol. The giving of this recipe to children of unspecified ages is, we respectfully submit, not only against the public interests but has a distinct element of danger.

We understand that this recipe is to be distributed in printed form by the end of the week and we make an urgent request to you to prevent this ill-considered action. The children and their parents would be quite mistaken in thinking that the resultant beverage produced by this recipe would be similar to that purchased legally and harmlessly in the shops.

We should be most grateful for an early reply as we would wish to delay further action until we hear from you.

I am, dear Sir,

Your obedient servant,

T.R.

Twickenham, Middlesex

20 December 1966

To: Mrs Doreen Stephens, [Head of Family Programmes] Television Centre, Wood Lane, W12

Dear Mrs. Stephens,

Last Saturday evening our two children, a boy aged 6 and a girl aged 4, watched the Dr. Who programme. This contained a sequence in which some of the main characters were threatened with hanging. I thought at the time that this part of the play lasted for a longer time than might be considered appropriate for a children's programme.

The following morning I was shaken to find that the children had hanged one of their dollies. Neither child is handicapped or emotionally unstable.

Children will people their own phantasies [sic] with a good deal of what they see on television and this includes violence. They are unable to detect the discord of implausibility and are much more ready than adults to accept things at their face value. Most of the violence portrayed is two dimensional – there is little depth to the emotion generated in the audience. Criminology between paper covers may be amusing; in real life it is sordid and depressing.

In my view, for violence to be acceptable on television for family viewing, it must be shorn of those qualities of horror, gruesomeness and sinister connotations which characterise real life. Our children are not old enough to understand the meaning of death, far less the ritual of hanging. I would be surprised if it had any more significance for them than a game of cowboys and Indians. But it is a game my wife and I would rather they did not play – the hanging of dolls I mean.

Yours sincerely,
Dr. T.N.

London SW1
23 February 1968

To: Thelma Cazalet-Keir [BBC Governor 1957–1962]
Dear Thelma,

Forgive me bothering you, but I know you used to be connected with the BBC, and I do not know who else to contact. I am very concerned at the hour 5.30 till 6 that a programme called Dr. Who is put on the screen. Last week I turned on this programme and a few minutes before it ended with a view to seeing the News my daughter aged 3 was in the room and watched. At the end of the programme a vast – by adult standards – terrifying monster appeared on the screen. The child became quite rigid with terror and ever since that evening we have to take her all round the house, search behind curtains etc before she goes to bed. She believes this monster is in the house – often screams 'Mama, mama don't go out there that man will get you.'

At her age it is just as easy for a monster to appear mysteriously in the house as on the screen. What I feel is that as little children must often look at television before 6 o'clock this frightening programme should not be put on till a little bit later.

See you before too long I hope –

Yours ever

[Lady] T.A.

Wakefield, Yorkshire
9 December 1963

To: The Director General, British Broadcasting Corporation, Broadcasting House, London W1
Dear Sir,

I am a parent of two boys aged 8 and 5. Last Saturday, I had the misfortune to view with my two boys what had in its first part promised to be a good adventure; Dr. Who. In its third broadcast it degenerated into a distasteful and horrific twenty-five minutes. A particularly horrible part was that where a man was mauled by an unseen but heard wild animal. It's [sic] effect on my five-year-old may be of interest. He is not an unusually sensitive or emotional child, but the night following the programme was a very unhappy one for him. During the programme he was particularly disturbed, as I imagine would any child of five seeing a badly clawed person moaning in agony.

I really cannot understand why the Producer thought it necessary to include such a sadistic scene. Surely it is possible to find gripping adventure stories which do not contain this sort of American Horror Comic type of thing. James Hilton's Lost Horizon' is an example.

What I am really curious about is the administrative machinery for deciding what is suitable for broadcasting when children of all ages are viewing. Judging by what was broadcast last Saturday between 5.15 and 5.40 this machinery needs badly overhauling.

Yours faithfully,

E. J. W.

Taunton, Somerset
29 September 1965

**To: The Controller, Children's Television,
B.B.C. Television Centre, London W12**

Dear Sir,

It was with a sinking feeling, superseded by something akin to disgust that I read of the return of the 'Daleks' in the serial 'Dr. Who'. Once again, the B.B.C.'s policy of 'If a programme appeals in it's [sic] first showing, repeat it until it's done to death' is evident. It is my opinion that 'Dr. Who' in general and the Daleks in particular represent the very dregs of Children's Television, and the fact that the programme does appeal to so many children is no excuse at all for repeatedly putting out such rubbish.

My husband wrote to you recently complaining of the low standard of Children's Television, but received a vague reply which did nothing to explain this low standard. I speak as the mother of two young children, and I can remember the very excellent 'Children's Hour' in 'Uncle Mac's' heyday. I think that television could produce programmes on the lines of [BBC radio's] 'Nature Parliament' and 'Regional Round'. Then there are well-known and well-loved series such as 'Toytown'. 'Winnie-the-Pooh' and 'Said the Cat to the Dog'. You have all the recordings lying idle (and most grievously so).

Perhaps you could devote two half-hours a week to programmes for boys (railways, aeroplanes etc.) and girls, (ballet, nursing etc.). I realise the difficulties of catering for a wide and differing audience, but too often Children's Television is put out to appeal to the masses, which means American cartoons and series, lots of pop music, and a generally poor standard. A bolder, better policy might attract far more viewers in the long run.

Yours faithfully,

P.M.P. (Mrs.)

Northfield, Birmingham

5 September 1967

**To: The Head of Children's Television,
B.B.C. Television Centre, London W12**

Dear Madam,

Some time ago I wrote to you to make several points of complaint about the Children's programmes that the B.B.C. were putting out. Subsequently, there was some improvement, with fewer American importations and the introduction of 'Jackanory'. Although it may have been accidental, my wife and I like to think we did have a hand in these changes. Since then the programmes have ranged from the good to the tolerable, but recently they have gone to rock-bottom.

On Sunday there was a repeat of 'Pinky and Perky' which my own daughters (aged 5 and 3) plainly recognised as a repeat and despised accordingly. On Monday there started a week's 'Jackanory' about the Second World War. When this programme first began it was declared as being intended for the under-sevens: it seems to me either a sophisticated or a nasty way of telling them stories to describe 'bombs falling and crushing them'. Gone are the naively innocent tales of Beatrix Potter and A.A. Milne and Rupert [the Bear]. Today, (Tuesday) your week hit rock-bottom. At a time when all six-year-olds might be expected to be watching, we were subjected to a new American cartoon; personally I consider this to be Trash. It is noisy and crudely done and it encourages all the worst excesses of American speech, linguist style and vulgar programming.

When my 6 year-old wrote to [conjuror and presenter] David Nixon in her best handwriting to say how much she likes his programmes and to ask for a photograph of Basil Brush, she did not receive so much as an acknowledgement. She has just recovered from the disappointment.

Yours faithfully,

M. P.

Northfield, Birmingham

23 March 1968

To: The Head of Children's Television,
B.B.C. Television Centre, London W12

Dear Madam,

Having just viewed this afternoon's episode of 'Dr. Who' I feel I must write to you again on this subject. Both my husband and I have written to you before questioning the suitability of this serial for children's viewing but I feel that this new story has entered a new area of unpleasantness. I am not against 'monsters' but the 'humanised' monsters such as the two men in to-night's episode strike me as belonging to a different category – horror for its own sake; and this is deplorable as well as being very frightening. In our case the solution is simple – one turns off the set, but I am worried about the number of children who are subjected to this sort of horror.

I think it is fair comment to say that the lingering camera shots of a menacing man with a fixed stare and bared teeth, of a gaping maniacal laugh, come all too close to the psychological horror of Orwell, Huxley or the Marat/Sade.

I am aware of the arguments for retaining this serial; apparently some children do like it although on the evidence of my own and various friends' children they can be terrified.

On a separate issue, may I again enquire if there is any hope of hearing the 'Children's Hour' recordings of Winnie-the-Pooh? These gave me very great pleasure as a child and I feel sure that children today would derive equal enjoyment.

Yours faithfully,

P.M.P. (Mrs.)

Wootton, Northampton

28 October 1962

To: The Postmaster General, House of Commons,
London SW1

Dear Sir,

I am gravely concerned about the choice of B.B.C. television children's programmes at the weekend. After maintaining a reasonable standard through the week they are often poor on Saturday and worse on Sunday.

After taking my family to Church on Sunday morning and to Sunday School in the afternoon, I am very happy for the children to see ten minutes of 'Sooty' type entertainment. But on the last two Sunday afternoons, failure to switch off promptly afterwards has confronted them with the spectacle of

   a) a grinning corpse with a knife handle protruding from its chest, and

   b) a close-up of a man receiving a sickening blow on the head; these were the opening scenes of instalments of a serial entitled 'The River Flows East'.

It may be that there is a place for this type of programme, but not at this time of day and not on a Sunday.

In my home the only result is the frustration of children deprived of expected entertainment. In other homes, irreparable damage may be caused to the minds of a rising generation. Children are being conditioned to accept violence as commonplace.

Is there any chance you can influence the Corporation in its choice of children's programme?

Yours faithfully,

G.D.S.

Cardiff

18 October 1959

To: The Director General, British Broadcasting Corporation, Broadcasting House, London W1

Dear Sir,

I have until now resisted the inclination to write to you concerning the increasing amount of American material shown on B.B.C. Television.

I feel however I must protest at the disgusting sadism and brutality portrayed in the first of a new series called 'Laramie'. We all know that the cinema industry is using this type of material at present in an attempt to halt the fall in attendances, but I would have preferred that the B.B.C. would refuse to set its sights at such a low level.

I am thinking in particular of the clubbing of a man – already on the ground – with a vicious blow from a rifle butt. The sound track emphasized the force, and if anyone believes a normal skull would withstand such an impact, the result may well be lethal.

Many parents of broad and progressive outlook, welcoming the treatment of many social problems in your excellent manner, are nevertheless being compelled to prohibit TV westerns in their family circles. Surely [early Hollywood silent cowboy star] Tom Mix and his old friends could entertain, thrill and excite us without disgust? Why not those who fill the screens of today?

Yours faithfully,

A.L.H.

B.Sc., A.B.Ps.S., A.M.B.I.M.

Atherstone, Warwickshire

13 October 1961

To: R.A. Butler M.P., House of Commons, London SW

Dear Sir,

I have on several occasions written to the Director of Programmes for the B.B.C. regarding the plays produced by the B.B.C. and have usually received a printed post card in acknowledgment of my letters. I am appalled by the programmes usually sent out between five and six o'clock on B.B.C. Television. These nearly always seem to include fights and shootings. One of the worst recently was a prolonged fight between two men in front of a cage in which a lion was pacing behind bars watching the combat. About two days ago there was an episode in which a man struck a woman in the face. These sort [sic] of exhibitions must surely encourage violence, and I think a great deal of the violent crime which is a growing menace to our society is due to them.

I think very careful consideration should be given to the selection of men responsible for the production of T.V. programmes most of which are insufferingly [sic] boring to me and of which the spoken word is usually in an unintelligible American drawl.

Yours very truly

E.W.M.

D.Sc. F.C.G.I. Hon. M.I.E.E.

Minsterley, Nr. Shrewsbury Salop

8 Jan 1963

To: The Director General of the B.B.C.

Dear Sir,

I have often watched with enjoyment the entertaining television programmes put out by your Corporation in which people like [cowboy star] Bronco Lane knock out their opponent with a hearty uppercut or a gangster stuns the detective with a sharp blow on the head with a revolver butt. The victim though is usually seen to rise within seconds and shake his head and carry on regardless.

I find, with concern, that children in this school believe that such blows to the head can be delivered with very little effect, whereas, of course, concussion, blindness, deafness or paralysis would be the most likely consequence in real life if death were escaped.

In view of the marvellous work you do in the cause of education I feel it would be reasonable to expect that this important aspect be stated by an announcer in children's viewing time, say perhaps 3 or 4 times a year.

Yours faithfully,

S.D.J.

Headmaster

CHAPTER TWO

THE ROYAL FAMILY

As can be seen from the appendix at the end of this book, the 1969 fly-on-the-wall documentary about the Royal Family was the second most popular programme on television in the 1960s. In an era of intense rivalry between the BBC and the ITV companies, when it was impossible to persuade the two to cooperate on the televising of major sporting occasions like the FA Cup Final so that viewers got the same event on both channels at the same time, it was a tribute to the uniqueness of the occasion that the Royal Family film went out first on BBC, since the BBC had made the programme, and was then repeated on ITV.

The Duke of Edinburgh had for many years wanted to modernise the institution of which he was a part. In 1968 Lord Mountbatten's son-in-law, the film producer Lord Brabourne, felt the Royal Family would benefit if it was seen by the public as being more modern and informal. This view was shared by the Queen's Australian press secretary, William Heseltine, and enthusiastically endorsed by Prince Philip. Brabourne suggested to him that a documentary should be made about the Royal Family's private life, recommending that Richard Cawston, then head of the BBC's documentary department, should direct the film. The time seemed auspicious as 1969 was the year of Prince Charles's investiture as Prince of Wales.

The Queen, had considerable reservations which were shared by both her daughter and her mother. Against the strong advice of the Queen Mother, however, the Queen was convinced by her husband and his uncle, Lord Mountbatten. She gave Cawston full access to Buckingham Palace, Windsor Castle, Sandringham and Balmoral for more than a year, shooting 43 hours of raw footage of the Queen's private and official life.

The result was a truly sensational 105-minute film which was avidly watched all over the world. Viewers were astonished to see the Queen in a headscarf driving the four-year-old Prince Edward to the village shop to buy sweets, astounded to see Prince Philip grilling sausages for a family picnic beside a Scottish loch and delighted to see Prince Charles snapping the A string of his cello against the cheek of his younger brother, Edward. It made them seem so homely, so ordinary, so ... well, just like us. The film was a global media event at a time when there were very few of them, yet by the end of the year of that first transmission, the Queen had come to appreciate the wisdom of her mother's initial advice and withdrew it from circulation. Apart from a short clip on YouTube which is repeated on various television documentaries, the film has not been seen in its entirety since 1969.

The Victorian constitutional historian Walter Bagehot had once famously counselled on the subject of monarchical mystique: 'We must not let in the daylight upon magic.' The 1969 film, despite its unanimously ecstatic reception, did exactly that and the Royal Family changed from a distantly waving symbol of British History into a family who were indeed just like us.

Perhaps unsurprisingly then, the selection of letters that follows there is a discernible pattern of increasing dissatisfaction with the monarchy and with its portrayal on television. There is nothing but rapture for the televising of the coronation in 1953 but, despite the widespread acclaim for Cawston's film, there is already a sense that the Royal Family were not entirely the same as imagination had previously made them. Perhaps being 'just like us', once the astonishment wore off, was not what their subjects wanted them to be.

It may also be that the work of the satirists had prepared the country for an alternative view of the Queen and her family. *That Was the Week That Was* lined up the monarchy as one of its constant targets as it also trained its weapons on the Macmillan government, the Church, Parliament and other institutions of state. The letters that poured into the BBC were invariably those of protest that the BBC, so long a part of the Establishment, should now take the side of those who wished to insult the monarchy. *TW3*'s successor, *Not So Much a Programme, More a Way of Life*, transmitted a sketch about the Duke of Windsor shortly after the death had been announced of his sister, the then Princess Royal, which drew a very large volume of complaints but the die was now cast. The Royal Family, who, as was frequently pointed out by the correspondents, could not defend themselves by answering back, were now a legitimate subject for mockery.

Undoubtedly, such lese-majesty was quite unimaginable in 1953 when the coronation of the young radiant Queen seemed to harbinger the dawn of a New Elizabethan Age.

THE CORONATION, 1953

The Radio & Television Retailers Association

21 June 1953

**To: The Chief Engineer, Television Service,
B.B.C. Alexandra Palace**

Dear Sir,

I have the honour to write to you on behalf of the Chairman and members of the Association in the County of Surrey to congratulate you and your staff for the very excellent presentation of the Coronation proceedings on June 2nd last.

Many viewers have told our members how very impressed they were by the high quality of the transmission which brought to them so vividly the Service in Westminster Abbey. The remarkable pictures of Her Majesty in the Abbey and during the processions, together with the clarity of sound on these occasions, has raised the status of television to a new level.

The wonderful results obtained are of course due to first class team work which in turn is possible only with correct management. The members therefore refrain from singling out any particular sector for special mention. It is agreed, we feel, that the remarkable close-ups of Her Majesty, and of the Prince Charles and Princess Anne at the window at Buckingham Palace, amongst many others could not have reached the screens of the receivers without the closest cooperation of the engineers in the transmission links.

It can fairly be said that the results of the broadcast have proved how completely right from all public points of view was the decision to televise the Coronation.

Thank you,

Yours faithfully,

E.B.L.

Ferranti Ltd., Hollinwood, Lancashire

5 June 1953

**To: Sir Ian Jacob, K.B.E., Director General,
B.B.C. London W1**

Dear Sir Ian,

I feel that I must offer you my congratulations on the splendid work of the B.B.C. Television Service throughout the day of Her Majesty's Coronation.

It would be difficult indeed to select any particular aspect of the work for especial mention. The disposition and use of the cameras within Westminster Abbey was brilliant, and I was most impressed by the maintenance of a steady level of sound volume at all points within the Abbey during the actual ceremony.

The camera units along the route of the procession were similarly used with very great effect, and the results were technically excellent under the rather poor weather conditions.

I am sure that those responsible for the administration, production and technical work are equally deserving of the highest praise.

Yours sincerely,

V.Z. de Ferranti

J, Arthur Rank Organisation Ltd, 38 South Street W1
5 June 1953

To: George R. Barnes Esq., British Broadcasting Corporation London

Dear Barnes,

I feel that I must write and congratulate you on the wonderful job that you did on Coronation Day in televising the Ceremony, and the procession etc. I saw every minute of it and I must say that I was completely enthralled.

Incidentally, I was very glad to think that you could only put on a black and white picture! This, of course, was a very selfish point of view. Nevertheless, my sincerest congratulations.

Yours sincerely,

John Davis
Managing Director

House of Commons, London SW1
4 June 1953

To: Major-General Sir Ian Jacob K.B.E. Broadcasting House W1

My dear Ian,

You will, I know, have been overwhelmed with congratulations over the B.B.C. Television programme on Coronation Day. I have heard nothing but loud and universal praise from all sections of the community – from the highest to the lowest. Having been in the Abbey myself I could not have appreciated more seeing on the T.V. in the evening all the bits one was unable to get a glimpse of in the Abbey.

In one of my hospitals for disabled men they were so impressed and overcome by the T.V. programme that they forgot all about the big party that they intended to have in the evening, and in some of the pubs in my constituency where they had expected some heavy drinking they found that everyone was glued to the T.V. set.

I know that in a job like yours you are apt to hear all the grouses and not much of the praise, but I am sure you should be highly delighted with the great appreciation for all your arrangements. I didn't hear any of the sound radio myself, but am sure it was equally good.

As you know, my Ministry is ceasing to exist very shortly, so I may either find myself back in the ranks of the wage earners again or precipitated into some other job.

All my good wishes,

Yours ever

Brigadier J.G.S.
V.C. M.C. M.P.

Ministry of Defence, Storey's Gate, SW1

3 June 1953

To: Lt.General Sir Ian Jacob K.B.E., C.B.,
Director General B.B.C.

My dear General,

I felt that I must drop you a short line to say that several members of the staff here have particularly remarked on the quite wonderful performance put up on the television programme yesterday (Coronation Day). My wife, too, who is by no means a television fan! particularly remarked on the amazing way the atmosphere and spirit of the Abbey got across in the television programme. Incidentally, my small son had the morning made for him when the cameraman 'caught' the Bishop who fell over.

I know how busy you are, so please do not bother to answer this letter.

Yours ever

R.E.
Secretary, Chief of Staffs Committee

P.S. Mr. Profumo rang. He wanted to tell you personally 'how wonderful the television was yesterday. It was absolutely staggering – I don't know much about the technical side of how the thing is done – I was viewing in the H of C with about 150 Ministers and people, and we were all terribly impressed.'

Ilkeston, Derbyshire
16 November 1963

To: The Director General, B.B.C.

Dear Sir,

TWTWTW

Having just listened to a particularly crude and offensive shaft of 'wit' directed against the Royal Family – I have switched off in disgust.

I had always thought the Royal Family was protected from such vulgarity by a Code of Conduct – apparently I was mistaken. That the B.B.C. does not enforce a better standard of 'entertainment' is highly deplorable – it was not always so, and the present tendency to allow 'dust-Bin' [sic] humour to be broadcast reveals a shocking lowering of standards. A much more rigid control over the 'Clever Young Men' is called for.

Yours faithfully,

G.S.D.

Ringwood, Hampshire
28 April 1963

**To: K Adam Esq. CBE, Director of Television,
Broadcasting House, London W1**

Subject: 'That was the week that was' on 27 April 1963

Dear Sir,

I write to record my disgust at the shocking reference made in the above programme to the 'Royalty of Europe'. I am personally a monarchist but whatever my views on this subject I am sure that the majority of decent minded people will consider that this item was not only disloyal and disrespectful to various Royal houses but it was in the lowest possible taste.

The visitors from Europe accepted an invitation from a Royal Princess of this country to attend the wedding of her daughter and a number of them were blood relations of not only Princess Marina but also Prince Phillip [sic]. The ridicule of these people, a number of advanced years, was disgusting enough, but to do so when they came to this country on the expressed invitation of a member of our own Royal House, it behoves all citizens of this country to show their customary respect.

Only a televised apology from you, sir, or at least the person responsible to Princess Marina and her guests can restore the renowned hospitality which this country has hitherto enjoyed. I would go further and call for the immediate resignation of the person concerned who is obviously totally unfitted to occupy such a position with an organisation where so much harm can be done by thoughtless action or was it intended to be a deliberate reflection on all Royalty?

I trust that this matter will receive your personal attention.

Yours faithfully,

N.V.B. (Lieut. Col.)

Hounslow West, Middlesex

28 March 1965

Dear Sir,

I was ringing your [Television] Centre on Sunday evening from 10.10pm until 11pm and got no reply. Did you give instructions not to answer the Phone during NSMAPMAWOL? Well, I think it was discusting [sic] dam discusting to put on that Program about the Duke of Windsor when his dear Sister was lying dead and he so ill himself. I think your Company is degrading and I am not looking in again. I shall get rid of the television and get out more.

All you talk about now is sex, dirty sex. Why don't you give up if you cannot find better material? Such stupid [sic] and a waste of time who the hell wants to look at such muck of no value to anyone.

Yours,

M. E. (Mrs.)

Sevenoaks, Kent
28 March 1965

Dear Sir,

I have never before been so incensed by a T.V. programme that I have tried to telephone from my home in the country to protest. I am sorry that your number was engaged, but not surprised, as no doubt hundreds of other decent citizens were also telephoning at the same time.

Whatever any of us may have felt about the abdication at the time, and whatever our feelings are now towards the Duke and Duchess of Windsor, I cannot imagine any programme in worse taste than yours.

As for that man, Frost, whether or not he devises these programmes he should be sacked. His smug smiles are sickening to decent folk.

To say that I am disgusted is a gross understatement. I sincerely hope that the volume of protests which you receive will result in a public apology, not only to the Royal Family, but also to such of your viewers as were unfortunate enough to have their sets still on after the news.

Yours faithfully,
R.M.V.

Reading, Berks.
29 March 1965

To the people who performed and allowed the viewing of the opera concerning the Duke and Duchess of Windsor I would like to say in my view all was in very poor and bad taste, stupid not in the spirit of English fair play, the performance was considering the sad loss of our Princess Royal most obnoxious to the extreme. However you lot have all had a fine education also of higher class than myself they didn't teach you Politeness costs nothing. I apologise for any bad spelling and maybe my written English. I am a poor hardworking old age pensioner.

C. G.

London SW3

29 March 1965

Dear Ned Sherrin,

A protest. I don't know if it is your fault or not, but I do think you should have insisted that the film on 'The Windsors' should have been taken out of 'Not So Much a Programme, More a Way of Life'. I had just switched over from I.T.V. who had announced that a special tribute to the Princess Royal would be transmitted after the Eamon Andrews Show, thinking the B.B.C. would also announce a similar programme, but to my utter horror and shock saw the film on the Windsors. I just couldn't believe it. I thought for a moment that the programme had been pre-taped so it would have been impossible to alter but if it was live, it was an utter disgrace.

I have never heard such nonsense – the B.B.C. saying they hadn't got time to alter it, surely some arrangement could have been made. David Frost could have discussed an extra subject to fill in the time. I think it was in pretty bad taste and most embarrassing – it put an awful clamp on the whole programme. Even Norman St.John Stevas normally so brilliant and witty seemed 'down'. It was most unfair to your cast and above all to the Windsors whom [sic] I am sure would have been delighted if it had been shown any other time other than a few hours after the death of the Princess Royal who untiringly gave so much of her service to the public.

Surely the B.B.C. could have made an effort.

Yours sincerely,

M.P.

London, SE1

Dear Sir,

So strong are my feelings on this subject that I had to write.

TV comic shows I like, but this week's performance in 'Death Us Do Part' [sic] was <u>disgusting</u>.

We are one of the few countries left, with a reigning monoch [sic], of which I am proud and there must be thousands of others, if they were honest.

As was said in the script, we haven't a great deal left out of the mighty country we once were, so please don't degrade one of the remaining few things [that keeps us] above most of the others.

Laugh, if we must at Politicians etc. but not the Queen, 'God Bless Her' and it wouldn't hurt if an apology was given by those concerned.

This is the first and last letter I shall write, hoping some one will do something about the Trash on some of these TV shows.

Sincerely,

(Mrs.) A.N.K.

North Mundham, Chichester
22 February 1967

To The Controller, BBC TV

Dear Sir,

When switching on BBC TV for the Panorama programme on Monday 20th February 1967 I was unfortunately a little early and saw the last few minutes of Till Death Us Do Part. I was horrified and disgusted to see what appeared to be a bottle of ink thrown 'accidentally' at a picture of H.M. The Queen. This was followed by loud laughter and this appeared to be the climax and the end of the performance.

I am sure I am not alone in decrying what I suppose is the attitude of the B.B.C. TV to the British Royal Family by this deliberate attempt to make fun of an institution that has benefitted this country so very greatly and at one who is not able to reply and who moreover was ill in bed at the time.

Yours faithfully,

P.A.B.N.

THE ROYAL FAMILY, 1969

Bodmin Moor, Cornwall
23 June 1969

From: the Princess Dolgorouky
To: Barbara Saxon, Production Assistant *Royal Family*

Barbara, it was tremendous – Truly an achievement and absolutely compulsive viewing. As you know, I am no monarchist but it brought very vividly the job they do as P.R. for Britain – and what a lot of work – despatch boxes, handshakes, interviews which are damned hard work even if pure formality!

Personally, I did not find her [the Queen] a pleasing personality – not a person one would like to know. But the rest of the family were really natural – even the kids glancing up at the camera! And I think the picture of Charles as a human is good.

What I want to know is how many feet of film were shot and scrapped – but it really is a triumph

BBC2 has at last reached Cornwall – now to see if we can get it – some places apparently are hopeless. Keep your fingers crossed.

Much love and we are expecting you soon.

Amersham, Bucks
22 June 1969

Dear Mr. Cawston,

You must have had a surfeit of congratulations, but I must say 'Thank You' for the most fascinating film I have ever had the privilege of seeing. There is only one adjective I can think of applying to it – fabulous.

Apart from anything else, I have seen the Queen in an entirely new light – and for all that I am most grateful.

Yours sincerely,

C. M.

Evening Standard, 47 Shoe Lane, London EC4
19 June 1969

**To: Richard Cawston Esq., Television Centre,
Wood Lane W12**

Dear Mr. Cawston,

I felt I really had to write and add a personal P.S. to what I have just finished writing for this afternoon's edition – to express my enjoyment and admiration of the Royal Family film we saw at the press screening. It is a tremendous feat to have brought off – I am sure the image of royalty will be changed more radically in 105 minutes than it has been in 105 years when it goes out on Saturday.

I am particularly happy to hear that the remainder of your material is going into the National Film Archive. Its presence there should give an excellent fillip to the appeal for funds which I know it's hoped to launch later on this year. I hope I live long enough to see it, too!

Yours sincerely,

Alexander Walker

Yorkshire Television, The Television Centre, Leeds

To: Richard Cawston

... and you needn't think (whatever the Mirror says) that just because She'll agree to be pushed around, that you'll get the same kind of co-operation from me ... After all, we do have a certain position to preserve.

Alan [Whicker]
PS: <u>Many</u> congratulations

National Viewers' and Listeners' Association
30 June 1969

**To: Richard Cawston, Producer 'The Royal Family' BBC
London**

Dear Mr. Cawston,

May I add the warm congratulations of this Association to the many expressions of appreciation which you have

doubtless received about your programme 'The Royal
Family'?

It was a wonderful film in every way and we are most grateful
for it.

Yours sincerely,

Mary Whitehouse (Mrs.)
Copy to The Press Secretary, Buckingham Palace

Longsight, Manchester
22 June 1969

Dear Sir,

May I express my thanks and delight for a wonderful showing
of 'Royal Family'? I watched every second of it in admiration and
thankfulness for having such a Royal Family.

Being a patriotic subject, I have seen as many of the Royal
Family as possible on my visits to London and when they have
honoured our City with their visits.

Your film, shown last night, made one feel we were in their
home with them and enjoying their holidays too!

Our Queen thrilled me with her happy laughter. Prince Phillip
[sic] and the children too made one feel it was just a normal
happy family.

I could go on and on with praise for your showing of such a film.

Please, please, let us have more of these intimate films of our
Royalty and Bless them for allowing it to be made.

Thank you a million times for this wonderful documentary
film and allowing me the proudest and happiest one hour forty
eight minutes of viewing for a long time.

I am,

Yours Truly,

E.W. (Mrs.)

Preston, Lancs.

27 June 1969

To: Mr. Paul Fox, Controller BBC1, Television Centre, London W12

Dear Sir,

Though late, my family and self would like to thank you, Mr. Richard Cawston and all staff concerned with the production, 'The Royal Family'. <u>Marvellous</u>. My son aged almost twenty three years exclaimed, 'Why I wouldn't have the Queen's job for a fortune. She works too hard and with hardly any personal freedom'.

Our Queen and Prince Philip with the Queen Mother as a Royal Family are a credit to Democracy in our own country and surely must impress other nations too. Their stability, sense of duty, impeccable manners, kindness with humour must make an impact too on the <u>weaker</u> members of the younger generation who experiment with drugs, sex and vandalism. These foolish young folk are really growing backwards to the animal state.

Our future King Charles proved in the interview with Cliff Michelmore he possesses both his Mother and Father's sense of duty, good manners and lively sense of humour. Thanks again, B.B.C.1.

Some time, please could you show a profile of Greta Garbo and a cycle of her films. Paul Robeson, Richard Tauber and of course Mantovani were also favourites of mine. May I add 'Blue Peter' improves all the time – lovely stories for children and adults too. Johnny Morris is great too. Also Ton Ton.

Many thanks,

Yours sincerely

H.M.A. (Mrs.)

Wonderburg II, Orteliusstraat 162, Amsterdam

28 September 1969

To: ITV and BBC, Mr Richard Cawston, London England

Dear Mr. Richard,

You and your team of workers my husband and I want to thank <u>very very</u> much for the most wonderful and touching picture may be you ever made!?

We were both very happy now to watch the real (as you know an expression of the Queen of England face help us the most!!!) And also her family life!! God bless you for all this, also your team of workers!!

Kindly regarding you and all of them.

Your most sincerely,

'FAN'

M. B.

22 September 1969

Dear Sir,

I just viewed your film 'Royal Family', it was a great film and good idea. I happen to be a FAN of the Queen. I was fortunate to see her while I was in Germany in 1965, while she was on tour there. And in London I saw the Rank film, 'The Queen Sees Germany' in color.

And in a 1953 issue of the 'DAILY SKETCH' 1 June 1953, I noticed the color film 'A QUEEN IS CROWNED'. These films would be nice to see on T.V. here in the U.S. I plan to ask CBS about these possibilities?

If in the future you could keep me posted on any such films to be viewed in the U.S. I'll appreciate it very much.

Keep up the good work –

Thank You

M. C.

Staff Sergeant

U.S. Army

Tennessee, USA 37212

1 October 1969

Gentlemen: I was very thrilled to see your program titled 'The Royal Family'. It was the most interesting program I've ever seen. This program was on television on September 21st 1969 on Sunday evening.

Would you have some pictures you could send to me of this program? I've been studying the Royal Family for a long time, and it's a very interesting study. Also, to look at all the pictures of the queen during her childhood, and to look at her as she is today with a fine family and such a very big job to do.

I'm very pleased that this program was in color, so all the uniforms and her dresses showed up on television, and all the dinners she has to attend all the time. I saw Her Majesty for my very first time, when the Queen and Prince Philip paid an official state visit as guests of Gen. and Mrs. Eisenhower in Washington (when Eisenhower was President Eisenhower.) I was very thrilled to see her [when] she visited the Eisenhowers on October 17 1957.

Thought you would be interested in this. If your office can send me some pictures of the program I would be delighted.

Is Her Majesty very nice about having your television crew filming the program, about her and her duties as Queen of England?

Thank You.

B. D.

London N8
3 August 1969

Dear Sir,

Due to my business I am unable to get out a great deal and rely on television for much of my entertainment.

I would like you to accept my sincere thanks for your 'Royal Family' film. This is one of the most enthralling and fascinating television films ever shown and was well worth the long hours and hard work that must have gone into the making of it. Films of this sort, which appear to be so few and far between, make a refreshing contrast to the violence that seems to be the dominating factor in so many programmes at the moment. I certainly look forward to seeing 'Royal Family' again when it is shown on BBC2 in colour.

Would you now please be kind enough to autograph the enclosed picture for my television scrapbook.

Thank you.

Yours faithfully,

H.T.

Newsagent, Tobacconist & Confectioner

London E17

13 August 1969

Dear Sir,

I wonder if you could clarify an argument for me. Some time ago you showed the famous 'Royal Family' programme. One sequence in this film showed the officers of the Royal Yacht Britannia who I understand are all Royal Naval Personnel toasting the health of the Queen. For this toast they stood, and yet as explained in your recent television documentary on the 'Captain of H.M.S. Bulwark', officers serving in the Royal Navy always sit for the toast because of an ancient tradition. Therefore could you please explain why the officers on the Royal Yacht stood for the toast.

Is there any specific reason or was it just for show for this one specific programme?

Please find enclosed a stamped addressed envelope. Hoping this does not inconvenience you.

Thanking you for a hopeful reply,

Yours faithfully,

J.C. (Miss)

Belfast

6 September 1969

Dear Sir,

Some time ago I wrote to the BBC Belfast expressing my appreciation of the film 'The Royal Family at Home' in Buckingham Palace. I expressed my appreciation of this film as a whole. I wish we had more on the same lines.

I did however query two points and the Belfast office said they would forward my letter (I am unable to remember the date) to the London office. I am rather disappointed that you have not seen fit to reply.

I would like to repeat my query. The diplomats, after they presented their credentials, turned their backs on the Queen and left the room. I was under the impression that when taking leave of Her Majesty, one retreated backwards making short bows as they went until they had [left] the room.

The other point is:- on board the Royal Yacht 'Britannia' the officers when toasting the Queen stood up to do so. I was [under the] impression that they remained seated.

This was a custom started by a King who, when he was Prince of Wales, bumped his head on a low beam when he stood up in response to a toast. He said this would cease when he was King, he kept his word and the custom of R.N. officers remaining seated has continued to this day. May I hope for your observations on this please.

Yours sincerely,

G.R.B.

THE ROYAL WEDDING, 1981

Stockton on Tees

2 August 1981

To: The Controller of Outside Broadcasts TV

Dear Sir,

The filming of last Wednesday's Royal Wedding was a delight – especially the service in St. Pauls.

However, many of my friends have commented as I have done too that we wished you could have filmed a little more of the Foreign Royal visitors and VIPs arriving in St. Pauls instead of going back time and again to the carriage driving down Fleet St. etc. You know the ladies really do enjoy seeing the fabulous fashions worn by these VIPs and our own Royal family. You hardly gave any coverage to this side of it – let's face it I am sure the majority of your morning audience was the ladies of the land!

Today, when the Sunday supplements came out I saw for the first time the superb flowers in front of St. Pauls – perhaps I missed these on TV or did you not show them? – if so what a great shame. So many of us get a great thrill from seeing the hours of work put into arranging wonderful floral displays.

Perhaps it seems wrong to write to you when Wednesday was such a wonderful TV spectacular but maybe you can bear my comments in mind for any future Royal wedding or occasion.

Yours sincerely,

J.M.D. (Mrs.)

P.S. I am not too keen on Angela Rippon's interviews – Sue Lawley would be my choice.

London N3

1 August 1981

To: The Head of Outside Broadcasting, B.B.C. Television

Dear Sir,

Now that you have had everyone patting you on the head for your Royal Wedding production may I as a person who likes to see all the pageantry simply ask!

What happened to the rest of the Queen's carriage procession to and from Buckingham Palace and St. Pauls? Going we saw the Queen's landau, a glimpse of the Queen Mother's but nothing at all of the 6 landaus which followed with their escorts.

Indeed your broadcast gave the impression that the Queen's procession consisted only of 2 landaus.

On the return we saw the bride and groom and the Queen with Earl Spencer. Nothing of the remaining landaus. Not even a sight of the Duke of Edinburgh with the bride's mother until they finally arrived at the Palace.

I await with interest your comments.

Yours Faithfully,

C. L.

Portsmouth, Hants.

30 July 1981

Dear Sir,

For years I have considered that the BBC were unrivalled in Outside Broadcasts etc.

I watched the covering of the Wedding on BBC and, to say the least, after weeks of promising the best pictures you made a complete hash of the whole thing.

1. Why did we not see the other members of the Royal Family in the procession?
2. The Pages were not seen until the balcony appearance.
3. The curtsey to the Queen by the Prince and Princess of Wales was almost missed.
4. We should have seen Personalities who were not picked out as they should have been. Even the Ring you almost missed.
5. Shots of Bells may be OK for New Years Eve but surely you had plenty to show. Whoever selected the Pictures to be shown should be banished to ITV for ever! I watched the highlights on ITV and all the points mentioned were covered by ITV. I think they won hands down.

The BBC is far too smug and they certainly did not get the best pictures yesterday. I will still watch BBC but please stop trying to be the eighth wonder of the world and concentrate on showing pictures of what the people wish to see.

Sincerely,

E.L.

Bristol

31 July 1981

To: The Director of Outside Broadcasting, BBC, London

Dear Sir,

We always switch on to BBC when there is an important event, as the wedding last Wednesday, and value the excellence of the production, but you seem to have camera men who were unsure of what they were doing especially in St. Paul's Cathedral. We never saw the members of the Royal family arrive or go to their seats, we were not told the names of the VIPs from overseas. We saw the bride come down and begin a curtsy to the Queen on her way out of the Cathedral and then for some reason known only to the controller we were once again switched to see the dome of St. Paul's. If he did it once he did it 20 times and became a laughing matter to those watching.

Because we were so very disappointed in your coverage of the event we switched to ITV in the evening and it was truly magnificent, we saw the full coverage of all we had hoped to see at the time. Tom Fleming was not as good as usual and did not tell us half as much as the ITV man did. I am sure I shall get your usual post card saying you received this letter and then silence. I do so understand it was a mighty day for you all and exhaustive rehearsals, perhaps too many, but you had been given much time to do it well and for the first time ever for a most important occasion you failed a bit.

Yours faithfully,

M.G.M.

P.S. The coverage of the actual wedding ceremony was beautifully done and so right and for that we thank you.

CHAPTER THREE

RELIGION

In the twenty-first century there is no doubt that the United Kingdom is a multicultural society. In the middle of the twentieth century Great Britain, as it mostly called itself then, would more accurately have been described as a Christian country. Many of the letters in this collection, which complain of deteriorating moral standards throughout television during the cultural revolution of the 1960s, refer to the country in this manner. Baby boomers who started school in the 1950s and 1960s saw few faces there that were not white. Schools made little or no provision for children of faiths other than Christianity.

The school day invariably began with an assembly which included Christian prayers and the singing of Christian hymns. Jewish children in state maintained schools, if there were sufficient of them, were allowed to withdraw from these assemblies when they moved from the 'parish notices' of regular school life to the daily service of worship. They were allowed to miss school during the Jewish holidays and to go home early on Friday afternoons during the winter, but if they knew what was good for them they did not draw attention to themselves. What had happened to the Jews of Europe was a recent memory.

The FM channel was not available at this time so the *Daily Service* was heard on the Home Service until the start of Radio 4, before it was relegated to the long wave where it now sits oddly alongside *Test Match Special*. The founding father of the BBC was Sir John Reith, a formidable six foot six inches tall, an unbending moralist the seventh son of an austere minister in the Church of Scotland. Informed that one of his announcers was getting divorced, Reith banned him permanently from ever reading the Epilogue again. The BBC's Christian principles derived from the influence of Reith and remained after Reith left the Corporation in 1938.

During the 1960s, the slot in Radio Four's *The Today Programme*, now called *Thought for the Day* and which reflects on topical issues from the perspective of faith, was called *Lift Up Your Hearts* and preceded the weather forecast and the 8 a.m. news. The difference in titles gives an indication of the difference in content.

The BBC was reflecting the centrality of Christian faith in the life of the country. Shops were closed on Sundays, which were regarded as a day for quiet contemplation. The decline in church attendance had already set in and certain sections of the church were seeking to engage with the social problems in their dioceses and parishes but, as far as the letter writers were concerned, people who called themselves Christians were expected to go to church as their parents and grandparents had. Whichever way they voted at a general election had no bearing on the expectation that they would continue to celebrate their faith. It was a Christian country and the BBC, particularly given its Reithian origins, had to conform in the programmes it produced. Reith had ordered the consecration of Studio 3E in Broadcasting House shortly after the building had opened so that the *Daily Service* could be broadcast from there every day.

Throughout the 1960s, the BBC maintained its commitment to religious programmes of a Christian nature but the people who made other programmes were starting to include 'clever young men' (and it *was* almost exclusively men) who had been to grammar school and university and wanted to make a splash in the attractive new world of television. One way they could do this was to thumb their noses at the Royal Family and at the established church. The chapters on Swearing and Bad Taste as well as this short one on religious programmes, tells of the reaction.

The Archbishop of Canterbury writes of his mystification because he doesn't have a television set. The Church of Scotland is equally and pardonably mystified as to why the BBC transmits programmes likely to appeal to its congregation at exactly the time on a Sunday when it is trying to get prospective worshippers out of their living rooms and into church. Many of the other responses to the blasphemies committed by comedy and satire programmes are contained in the chapters dealing with those programmes.

Lambeth Palace London SE1
2 November 1957

To: C. Beadle Esq. C.B.E. [Head of Religious Broadcasting] Broadcasting House London W1
Dear Mr. Beadle,

When I get complaints about things on T.V., I am in a hopeless position as I do not possess a set, and the only time I see T.V. is when I am staying in somebody else's house. But I have received a complaint which I think I ought to pass on to you. It comes from Oxford and is a criticism of the T.V. programme on Tuesday night last at 10.35. The writer says:

'It was called Life Line. The three debaters were good and respectful and dignified. The 4th person, apparently a recent undergraduate and now a Don at Christ Church, behaved disgracefully. He derided the idea of the Incarnation, the Resurrection. He described the Creed as mumbo-jumbo, he ridiculed the Communion Service and was blasphemous about the holiest and most precious beliefs of Christians which he said were no doubt good enough for ignorant peasants of long ago.

I have learned to distrust many of these complaints which reach me – on the other hand sometimes there is something in them, and all I can do is to ask you whether you would look into this particular criticism and let me know whether there is any justification in it or whether it is just the reaction of a person too easily shocked.

Yours sincerely
Geoffrey Cantuar
[Geoffrey Fisher, Archbishop of Canterbury]

The Church of Scotland, George St., Edinburgh
27 December 1963

To The Controller BBC Scotland, Queen Margaret Drive, Glasgow

Dear Mr. Stewart,

I am instructed by the Church and Nation Committee to write to you seeking information on the following two matters.

1. Sunday Morning Educational Broadcasts

In view of the fact that certain education programmes are being transmitted on Television at an hour when many prospective viewers in Scotland are attending Church, would it be possible for these transmissions to be repeated on another day of the week or at an alternative time? The programmes on Crafts and Skills (Home Dressmaking etc.) on Sundays 11.45 am – 12 noon have been specifically mentioned to us.

2. BBC 2

(a) Could you advise the Committee as to whether the National Broadcasting Council for Scotland will have the same powers for BBC 2 as it now has with BBC (TV)?

(b) Who will be responsible for religious broadcasts on BBC 2?

(c) Will the 'closed period' on Sundays, 6–7.30p.m., operate also on BBC 2?

The Committee is aware that BBC 2 will not come to Scotland for some time yet, but if it were possible for you to give us some information and guidance on these points, it would greatly help us in making our report to the Church of Scotland and we would be very grateful.

Yours sincerely
T. M.

Crawley, Sussex
9 Dec 1966

Dear Sir,

I have watched your school programme '1940' today. One part of the film was of a starving Jew lying in the street with people walking by without taking the slightest notice of him. The commentary was that the German people had given their conscience to Hitler and did not care any more what happened to other people.

I am Austrian by birth. I was ten years old when Austria was annexed to Germany and the Jews in my hometown left. They sold their belongings in an orderly fashion and I remember that we felt very sad for the people who had to leave their homes. One family returned from America after the war and are living happily in that town again. I never saw a starving Jew anywhere in the streets. We knew that concentration camps were awful places but no one really knew what went on inside them any more than the people of Shepherd's Bush know what goes on inside Wormwood Scrubs.

[There was] no mention of the suffering the German people had to go through when their towns were bombed far, far worse than London ever was. I am thinking particularly of the terrible air raid[s] on Dresden. There was no mention of the many cripples and the suffering of the German and Austrian people after the war when there was no food, no fuel, no jobs and so many were homeless. I could tell of some things the Russians did in Austria.

I think it is a great pity that children in this country are brought up with all this hatred of 20 years ago. If you have to show films like '1940' I think you should show them late at night at least and let the children grow up unbiased and unprejudiced.

Yours faithfully,

Mrs. I. B.

Crawley, Sussex

28 Dec 1966

To: Mr. Kenneth Adam, BBC Television Centre, London W.12

Dear Mr. Adam,

Thank you for your reply to my letter on the programme '1940'. I am sorry I have to write once more because it is quite obvious that you did not read my letter properly.

My intention was not to minimise the happenings in concentration camps but to show how little ordinary people knew of what went on. My former French teacher did actually help a Jewish lady to leave Austria. Concentration camps were understood to be for political prisoners. You don't need to tell me that I ought to know of the atrocities which were committed against the Jewish people. I do know NOW but I did not know BEFORE 1945 and neither did any of my friends and relations in Austria and Germany. We feel very sad indeed that people of our country were capable of these crimes but that does not make 80 million of German speaking people guilty for the murders that were carried out by a few thousand fanatics. [O]ne would think there had been a poster up in every German town 'Come and watch the execution of the Jews' or 'Free trips around the gas chambers'. These killings were done in the greatest secrecy and I fail to understand how one can accuse people of having let things happen when they did not even know what was going on. The camps were visited by International Red Cross officials which goes to show that even [they] do not have a chance to find out everything or else these killings could not possibly have taken place.

'Truth will out' is an old saying. It came out what happened in the concentration camps; it will also come out there are millions of decent German and Austrian people who had nothing to do with any crimes whatsoever.

Yours sincerely
Mrs. I. B.

West London Synagogue, Seymour Place, W1
6 May 1968

To: The Controller of Programmes, B.B.C. Television, Television Centre, Wood Lane, London W12
Dear Sir,

I am writing to you in connection with the programme 'The State of the Jews' broadcast on 2nd May and to register my strong personal criticism and protest over the way in which the Jewish community in this country was portrayed.

As a string of clichés was being unravelled, it became increasingly difficult to see the point of the programme. It showed some of the worst features of Anglo-Jewish life – some standard footage of Israel. Not a word was said about the contribution of Jews and Judaism to the social, political, scientific and cultural life of this country. And to have social welfare activities portrayed by a bread line in the East End is a gross distortion of the much positive realities. It was also regrettable that Mr David Wheeler had to go to California to get the one articulate contribution on Reform Judaism –there are some 45,000 progressive Jews in this country who were completely ignored.

If there were regular programmes on Jewish life I would just let it go as another programme that did not come off. But since there are no more than three or four hours of programmes dealing with this subject in any given year, I must express my deep regret at having lost an opportunity for an intelligent presentation. I trust that the B.B.C. will find it possible to set right this situation by showing some of the other and infinitely more wholesome aspects of our community's life and problems, its aspirations and achievements.

Yours faithfully,
Rabbi Hugo Gryn

Anglo Jewish Association
14 October 1963

Dear Sir,

I should like to preface this letter with a comment that neither I personally nor this Association is over sensitive to references to Jews in popular entertainment.

I was, however, somewhat disturbed and surprised by the edition of *Z Cars* on October 9th.

For no understandable reason the principal character, an aggressive, cowardly young man, was eventually disclosed as a Jew and his father was portrayed with a foreign accent and questionable business morals.

There was some vague attempt to explain the young man's aggressiveness by virtue of the fact that he was suffering from a strong inferiority complex, because he was a Jew and, indeed, the story carefully described his father's non acceptance by local society. The psychology of the piece was so shallow and out-dated that in a popular programme of this kind it might well have done considerable harm.

The foreign accented Jewish businessman is a generation or two out of date and to explain away nasty social attitudes as a result of Jewish background is an insult to the Anglo-Jewish community. Most young Jews from similar backgrounds are not nasty and if they are it is absurd to ascribe their nastiness to their Jewishness. Perhaps the writers were after a little local colour to make the characters more interesting. There certainly seemed no other reason why they should be Jewish.

Yours faithfully,

C.S.

CHAPTER FOUR

COMEDY

When discussing the BBC's comedy programmes of the 1960s it is understandable that much of the attention is focused on the innovative series: *Hancock, Steptoe and Son, Till Death Us Do Part*, Spike Milligan's *Q* programmes, *Dad's Army* and *Monty Python's Flying Circus*. Although *Dad's Army* hardly feels groundbreaking now and is still a staple of BBC2's Saturday night schedules, it was brought to air in the teeth of opposition from Paul Fox, the Controller of BBC1, who thought it would be regarded as offensive by those who had lived and fought their way through World War II.

It should, however, be remembered that the majority of comedy on BBC television at the time was cosy and unthreatening – Harry Worth, Dick Emery, Benny Hill, Eric Sykes and Hattie Jacques, *Marriage Lines* with Richard Briers and Prunella Scales and *All Gas & Gaiters*. That is why *Till Death Us Do Part* aroused such fury when it was first transmitted as a series in June 1966 (just in time for Alf to celebrate the winning of the World Cup by West Ham United) after a pilot episode in the *Comedy Playhouse* strand – which was the way *Steptoe and Son* had started four years earlier.

In both cases, what was at the heart of the characters' conflict was the struggle between the ideas espoused by the different generations. In *Steptoe and Son*, Harold Steptoe (Harry H. Corbett) was a supporter of Harold Wilson, the Labour Party, political reform and upward social mobility. His toothless father Albert (Wilfrid

Brambell), a World War I veteran, was a staunch Conservative and monarchist whose emotional neediness prevented any of Harold's dreams being realised. In *Till Death Us Do Part*, Alf and Else Garnett essentially played out the same generational war with their daughter Rita and Mike, their long-haired Scouse layabout git of a son-in-law played by Antony Booth.

Steptoe was criticised for its 'dirty' setting in the junkyard of a Shepherd's Bush rag and bone business, so different from the domestic tranquillity and sitting-room sofa of traditional British sitcoms. Despite his aspirations, Harold is frustratingly shackled to the 'dirty old man' set in his greedy ways, so their relationship contains considerable pathos. *Steptoe*'s creators, Ray Galton and Alan Simpson, were more interested in character than social analysis; *Till Death* contains much more raw anger. Creator Johnny Speight based Alf Garnett on his East End docker father, whose unreconstructed racist views had caused him considerable anguish.

So it was ironic that, confronted by a bad-tempered, ignorant, racist, sexist, foul-mouthed chauvinist, the British public should take him to their hearts. It was the very reverse of what Speight had intended, but the instant and enormous popularity of the show indicated that Speight had touched a prominent nerve in British society. Less than two years after the first series began transmission, Enoch Powell made his 'Rivers of Blood' speech and East End dockers marched in support claiming 'Enoch Was Right'.

The working class of East End London had previously been portrayed as the salt of the earth and Cockney sparrows, stoically picking up the pieces after the latest Luftwaffe raid, singing music hall songs in the Tube during the nightly Blitz, and unfailingly cheerful at all times. It was a shock to television audiences to see a realistically presented working class family so bitterly divided, with parents who should be setting an example to the children instead portrayed as ignorant and stupid.

Alf and Else thought they were doing the right thing – standing up for the monarchy and the Tory Party, idealising Winston Churchill and the Empire, but their battles with their progressive children were not just ideological but generational and cultural. Mike and Rita were relaxed about immigration and the new sexual mores which Alf and Else believed threatened the foundations of society, as did the new music, films, fashions and hairstyles.

It wasn't so much the ideas that Alf embraced which so infuriated the letter writers as the language he used in trumpeting their values. Alf used 'bloody' and 'bleeding' to an extent that had never been heard before on television, even though the BBC desperately traded with the writer (whom they were very unwilling to lose), offering, for example, to keep two 'bloody's if he would cut another 'bleeding'.

Alf, of course, was an admirer of Mary Whitehouse. Her public disparagement of the programme merely provoked Speight to write an episode in which Alf is seen reading a book written by the doyenne of the Clean Up TV Campaign. Teased by Mike, who can't stand Whitehouse, Alf expostulates why he is reading her book, 'She's concerned for the bleedin' moral fibre of the nation!' The episode ends with the book being burnt.

Nottingham
16 January 1966

Dear Sir,

I wish to make strong complaints against the showing of the programme 'Till Death Us Do Part' on B.B.C. Television.

It is a programme which plumbs the deaths [sic] of vulgarity in its references. Since it lacks humour, it is not entertainment but a cheap way of getting the audience's attention by shocking them.

I teach in a deprived and poor area of Nottingham where the parents lack discrimination in allowing many young children of 6,7,8, 9 and 10 years of age to watch such filth on television. Many of the children use such references as 'silly old Moo' and 'you old cow' in the classroom. References which they have obviously adopted 'From Death Us Do Part'[sic]

Do not forget that children are influenced by the programmes they see on television as well as by the teacher in the classroom.

The teacher in a deprived area has a continuous battle to uphold morals and standards of decency. While [sic] make our battle more difficult by allowing these indecencies on television, especially at an hour when many children are still watching?

I am sure I speak for many others as well as those in my profession when I ask for this programme to be withdrawn.

Yours truly,

H. B.

Surrey

27 February 1967

Dear Mr. Wheldon,

I have just spent fifteen minutes trying to speak to the Duty Officer regarding the lamentably low standard of 'Till Death Us Do Part'. I am told that, in order to have a written reply to my complaint, I must 'write in'. I am writing direct to you, as I don't ever 'write in' to or for anything.

The programme must be expunged from the B.B.C. This evening we have been subjected to a low standard of viewing which centred around a lavatorial humour and which had a strong anti-coloured bias. In England today, when everything is being done to integrate races, your programme has done more, in thirty minutes, to undermine all that has been worked for to achieve this integration in the past years.

Quite apart from this, there are many teenagers who, having finished their evening's homework, look forward to some entertainment at the end of their day's work. It is quite impossible to classify this programme as entertainment; and in fact, I contend that it can only be classified as degradation in the extreme.

I shall look forward to your assurance that 'Till Death Us Do Part' has been firmly put into the place which it deserves – the dustbin – and that it will not be foist on the public any more.

Yours truly,

P. G. M.A. Oxon.
Headmaster

National Viewers & Listeners Association
21 September 1972

To: Rt.Hon. Lord Hill of Luton, Chairman, The BBC, London W1

Dear Lord Hill,

I felt it only appropriate that I should send to you a copy of the letter written today to Sir John Eden. It does, of course speak for itself. I would only add that to have recourse to such language and ideas serves also to underline the paucity and tawdriness of the programme.

Yours sincerely,

(Mrs.) Mary Whitehouse

National Viewers & Listeners Association
21 September 1972

To: Rt.Hon. Sir John Eden MP., Minister of Posts & Telecommunication

Dear Sir John Eden,

During the course of Wednesday night's episode of 'Till Death Us Do Part' there was a conversation between the characters about the birth of Jesus Christ. The general trend was as follows:

Mary could not have been a virgin as God was the father of her son and the characters wondered how 'they (up there)' 'did it'. Did they 'do it' like we do? And why had Mary conceived only one child? Was it because she was 'on the pill'?

I hope you will agree that such talk was not only obscenely blasphemous, but a calculated offence to a great many viewers.

It is abundantly obvious that the present Governors are unable, or unwilling, to effectively fulfil their role as 'trustees' of the public interest and the need for someone capable of dealing with recalcitrant writers and producers becomes ever more urgent.

Yours sincerely,

(Mrs.) Mary Whitehouse

Richmond, Surrey
15 January 1968

To: The Director General, BBC.

Dear Sir,

You may be interested to have the following comments which I have extracted from a letter received from a middle-aged, middle-class friend in Sweden last week. A propos of current events in Britain she writes: 'I was a bit anxious until I saw Till Death Us Do Part this afternoon. England is a wonderful country to produce such wonderful programmes. We are getting more and more TV programmes from England, and many of them are extremely good and they get very good reviews; many of them have quite hard social criticism.'

I thought last week's programme of the Garnett family did more to root out false unscientific ideas about blood, race and heredity than any number of earnest biology programmes and though most of the people who voted for the programme in Talkback wouldn't realise this perhaps the next time they find themselves expressing this sort of belief they <u>may</u> feel uncomfortably like little Alfs and little Elses and stop to think a moment. I am glad the family were their real nasty selves last week. Sometimes, unfortunately we see too much of the lost little man in him (Alf) and this rouses dangerous sympathies which may get attached to his prejudices. Else is always formidably stupid and never, by a flicker, suggests she has any heart or mind. May I suggest that a new series might seriously send-up the not-so-darling dodos from other ranks in society? Unfortunately the approach there nearly always loses its edge.

Yours faithfully,

E. H.

Monmouth

18 January 1968

**To: Huw Wheldon, Head of B.B.C. Television,
Broadcasting House, LONDON W1**

Dear Sir,

On March 28th of last year I wrote to you regarding the programme 'Till Closing Time Do Us Part', and expressed the very real concern which I shared with others over the type of material being screened, and I received a very courteous reply from Miss. Kathleen Haacke.

I am very sorry to have to write again, particularly in view of the fact that once more it concerns the same Author and Cast, for the programme which was screened in which the Heart Transplant operations and Blood Donors came in for ridicule, is to say the least in very bad taste, coupled with the bad language which Mr. Speight sees fit to use in his so-called comedy put over by Mr. Garnett & Co.

This sort of material is alien to B.B.C. Television standards, and after watching the programme 'Talkback' last Sunday evening, I am compelled to register my protest in view of what was said, and it was a very sad reflection to hear a coloured fellow human being say that the immigrants thought that we had something to offer them in Great Britain, but this was not so after seeing the disgusting behaviour and comments by Garnett at the Blood Donor session.

[W]e here in Wales do not subscribe to this low level of comedy, and I hope that in future programmes that references to the Queen and Royal Family and also to the Prime Minister will be cut out, as this would not be allowed in any other country and personally I do not consider these 'jibes' as becoming to our country of which we are very proud to belong.

Yours sincerely,

H.G.L.

Liverpool 13

27 December 1966

To: Director Religious Broadcasting, B.B.C. Television, London W12

Dear Sir,

I wish to draw your attention to a programme broadcast on Channel 1 at 7.0 p.m. on Boxing Day under the title 'Till Death us do Part' which must have been offensive to many thousands of Christian people who treat the Christmas Festival with the significance it deserves.

The dialogue was in every sense one of bad taste apart from the continual use of the adjective 'bloody' and the vulgar word 'pollock' [pillock? bollocks? what is vulgar about a fish or a South African cricketer?] The segment concerning the religious aspect of Christmas bordered on the blasphemous. The programme moreover was shown at a peak viewing time when a large number of children – as my own daughter – would be viewing.

I appeal to you to take this matter up immediately with the producer concerned so that nothing of this objectionable nature be shewn [sic] again at a time when the B.B.C. ought to be endeavouring to maintain a true sense of values. Is there nothing that can be done to curb this type of producer from being let loose upon a vast audience on Boxing Day? I personally looked for entertainment yesterday evening not a vulgar intrusion into a low-down row between a man and his wife; as you may well realise, I can go to homes in my area every day of the week if I wish to witness such scenes.

I hope to have a favourable reply from you and an assurance from the B.B.C. that such a programme will be entirely banned in the future.

Yours sincerely,

E.R.

Minister

Liverpool 13

13 January 1968

**To: Mr. Huw Wheldon, B.B.C. Television Centre, London
W.12**

Dear Mr. Wheldon,

About twelve months ago we had some correspondence
concerning 'Till Death us do Part'. I protested a particular
edition screened on Boxing Day 1966 and I accepted your reply
though I found your comments in favour of the programme
pretty thin.

I now write you again in the strongest possible terms
regarding the same programme shewn [sic] last evening.
I have scarcely ever witnessed a programme in such bad
taste and the general tone was offensive even to the most
hardened. Why must we have to tolerate the obscenities, the
vulgarities and the language of Mr. Alf Garnett? In your letter
to me last year you used the phrase 'delight and please' as
the general verdict on the programme. All I can say is that
if such a programme delights and pleases then the audience
giving such a verdict must be depraved in mind. You remark
in your letter, there is a delicate line to be drawn, and I
heartily agree, but I would emphasise without personal malice
that the responsibility is yours and you failed miserably to
exercise that responsibility last evening. Surely your job as
an organisation is not pander to the lowest tastes but point to
the highest. Those whose taste is in the gutter and the dustbin
should not be catered for by a public corporation and I hope
something will be done at once to have the whole matter re-
considered.

Kind regards and thank you for your personal reply last time.
Yours sincerely,
(Rev.) E.R.

Hatton Derby

28 March 1967

To: the Director of Television BBC Television Centre London W12

Dear Sir,

On Easter Monday evening I did not realise that the usual 8.50pm news bulletin was scheduled ten minutes later and was accordingly regaled with some ten minutes of 'Till Closing Time Do us Part'. I must confess that main thought was that the magnificent resources which the B.B.C. undoubtedly has available were being utterly prostituted on such trivial drivel. When one thinks back and remembers such wonderful programmes as The Black & White Minstrel Show and many other really enjoyable shows, and then is faced with the incoherencies of such a production as this, one almost prefers the 'kitchen sink' rubbish that is at least driving a point home to those who care to think it over. Was that really the best you could find for a holiday evening?

On the other hand, when its next run comes around, may I add my plea to the many you must surely get, that Going for a Song should be allocated rather more time. Not, please, a change of time, but simply a longer period for our enjoyment of this urbane and civilised conversation piece, which so many of my friends enjoy so much.

Yours faithfully,

(Rev.) D. H. B.

Nottingham

3 November 1965

To: Kenneth Adam, Director of Programmes, BBC Television

Dear Mr Adam,

I have just read in the local paper of the adverse remarks made to you re 'Steptoe & Son'. I think it one of the best items and certainly much less harmful than many of these murder films. My advice to the ladies who spoilt your meeting is – 'If you don't like it, turn it off'.

I do not often 'look in' except for nature films and the news but I look forward to the excellent acting and humour of 'Steptoe'. Long may it go on.

Yours truly,

S. O. (Mrs.)

Greenford Middlesex
4 November 1965

Steptoe & Son etc.
Dear Sir,

I had to write to you after the Local Conference of Women's Organisations, including the Mothers Union, had criticized Steptoe and Son and other Programmes which appear on Television.

I am in my middle 70s. I started life as a School Teacher, but, through no fault of my own, I had to abandon the career I had anticipated. So I came from the country to live with my aunt and uncle. He told me the best way to find my way around London was to observe people and places wherever I went too. In that way one learns a lot. I think the Mothers Union is too local in its calculations although it does good work.

We here enjoy Steptoe & Son. It is so like real life. I know my husband, an Old Contemptible and ex-Gunner would enjoy it.

We also, my Son and I, enjoy Z Cars as my brother-in-law is a retired Policeman. Also Dock Green [sic] and many other of your programmes.

Those things we do not want to view, we just leave out. It is as easy as that. Please keep up the good work in trying to please most of us.

And to finish with I must thank you for The Great War series. Of course it made some of us older ones cry. But we would not have missed it for anything.

Yours faithfully,

Mrs. E. S.

CHAPTER FIVE

DRAMA

The same social events which influenced the start of groundbreaking comedy also created the atmosphere in which innovative drama flourished at the BBC. In the late 1950s all departments of the BBC seemed to be transfixed by the glare of the ITV headlights. The commercial network not only transmitted high-ratings American imports like *77 Sunset Strip* and *Dragnet* but outflanked the BBC by originating domestic dramas like the strand of plays which were screened under the umbrella title of *Armchair Theatre*, and of course *Coronation Street* which Granada started transmitting in 1960.

Armchair Theatre had been running for two years when the Canadian Sydney Newman arrived in 1958 to supervise it. As a North American, he had not been raised with the reverence for the legitimate theatre which effectively had been the case with most BBC drama producers and directors. As a consequence, he was much more anxious to seek work from living playwrights like Harold Pinter, Clive Exton and Alun Owen, whose first television plays were transmitted by ABC, having been commissioned by Newman. The influence of John Osborne, Arnold Wesker and the so-called Angry Young Men in the theatre and commercial successes in the cinema like *Saturday Night and Sunday Morning*, *Room at the Top* and *A Kind of Loving*, which drew their inspiration from contemporary events, had left the BBC drama department hopelessly fossilised.

The BBC responded to its isolation by poaching Newman from ABC and encouraging him to open the BBC to new influences. Under his aegis, the BBC developed *Z Cars*, which included among its writers Troy Kennedy Martin, Alan Plater, John Hopkins and Allan Prior. All used their learning experience on *Z Cars* to progress to significant careers. Plater went on to write *The Beiderbecke Trilogy*, Troy Kennedy Martin wrote *Edge of Darkness* and Hopkins graduated from *Z Cars* to write the award-winning quartet of plays, *Talking to a Stranger*, before moving into films and life in California.

Newman expanded the personnel and reach of the drama department, sidelining the old hands of BBC Drama who preferred another stab at Rattigan or Chekov to anything more challenging, and encouraging young people who wanted to make his sort of contemporary drama. He despised the BBC's taste for plays about the upper classes who, he pointed out rather acidly, didn't watch television, probably didn't own television sets and whose activities would not exactly resonate with the working class and the people who formed the basis of the general television audience. Under Newman the BBC produced plays, series and serials that responded to the seismic changes in British society in the 1960s.

The Wednesday Play tended to be where Newman took the most chances and which created the most controversy. Occasionally Newman's creative boldness met with resistance higher up the BBC chain of command. In 1965, Peter Watkins wrote, produced and directed *The War Game*, a film depicting the aftermath of a Soviet nuclear attack. It was around the time that Hollywood produced both *Fail Safe* and *Dr. Strangelove*, which essentially dealt with the same nightmare scenario and were critically acclaimed, but it frightened the life out of both the BBC and the government and was not screened for twenty years.

Under Newman, BBC Drama showed itself willing to tackle almost any subject but its new brashness inevitably produced howls of outrage from those who now regularly objected to anything new on the BBC. *Cathy Come Home* showed to an ignorant public the terrible social effects of homelessness; *Up the Junction* was an unflinchingly honest depiction of a backstreet abortion and working-class life in Clapham in general; *Culloden* was praised by the critics for its realism and loathed by its opponents for its depiction of the brutality of battle.

By the middle of the decade it was becoming possible to predict with unerring accuracy which subjects would attract the greatest hostility. Anything that involved religion or sex was bound to provoke complaints. Interestingly enough, there are almost no letters at all complaining about *Cathy Come Home*. Perhaps the sheer horror of it, especially the ending when the two children are dragged away from their mother by unfeeling social workers, stunned the nation into a shamefaced acceptance that the play merely dramatised what had been staring the country in the face for years but which had been studiously ignored.

In a sense, Garnett and Loach's film was the perfect example of what drama could do and, for all its perceived shocking innovation, it simply held a mirror up to nature and showed society its own image – as it had been doing for four hundred years. The complainants thought otherwise, of course, and did not wish those images to pour uninvited into their living rooms. Fortunately, all they could do was to write the letters, not of all of which were condemnatory.

Edgware, Middlesex
11 October 1962

Dear Sir,

Regards the BBC Play Stamboul Train I wish to say I only wish there was more of them. I didn't see any thing wrong or disgusting.

My son seen it 18 years old and my grandchild 12 years.

Believe me, sir, I wouldn't like your job. You have some thing to put up with. You can't please every one I don't suppose.

If these people (Vicar included) didn't like it they should put it off. I dare say they have the other channel to switch to. I get so mad at them so-called grown up people complaining. Let people watch what they want or turn it off.

A few more plays like that mentioned and Z Cars and of course Step-Toe another very good programme. I will be very pleased when that comes back.

Some of them had to have a crack at Z Cars pulling it to pieces. I like Z Cars and my family and 20 relations can give you the names if you require them the actors are first class every one perfect. We get a good laugh at the Scot and the sergeant behind the desk. Please don't ever take notice of people I beg of you as we can't wait till Z Cars comes on. Every thing is left in the house till our family sees Z Cars and the Sunday repeat. I never get tired of seeing Z Cars.

Hope I don't bore you with my writing and my bad spelling.

I remain

Again

Yours sincerely

Mrs A.

Tenby

Boxing Day 1958

To: The Director General, The B.B.C., London

Dear Sir,

I cannot think what evil genius persuaded the B.B.C. to put on the Christmas night play 'The Black Eye'. For a stark combination of inanity and immoral living I can imagine nothing worse. That the fortunes of a family and of an 'angry young man' can be restored by a drunken resort to chance is a representation that can speed up the decline of our country.

Certainly, the time is come where those who direct the great instrument of television in this country should have a greater sense of responsibility.

Another amazing thing to me is the way in which the liquor trade is outsmarting the B.B.C. For their advertisements on I.T.V. they presumably have to pay a fairly heavy charge: but the B.B.C. is gratuitously advertising the drink trade on a very great proportion of its programmes by making it, however unnecessarily, appear to be a sine qua non of social life.

Hundreds of boys, girls, young men and young women are getting into very serious trouble owing to drink. It is a contemptible thing that so important a national instrument as BBC Television should be aiding their downfall.

Yours faithfully,

(Rev.) D.T. (M.A.)

Postman's Piece, The Wold, Claverley, Nr. Wolverhampton
1 January 1961

To: Sydney Newman, Head of Drama, BBC Television, London W12

Dear Mr Newman,

But for the Christmas celebrations I would have written earlier to say how pleased we were to read that your department had decided not to show any more 'kitchen sink' plays. To those of us, like myself, who have a deep loyalty to the B.B.C. because of what it has done in the past and what it could do again, for the nation, this decision brings considerable relief and satisfaction.

Please do not feel that we wish to turn our backs on the more difficult, unpleasant aspects of life, but what most people want to know is how to deal with them! To write and produce plays that do this with fun, insight and real imagination would present our young – and old! – playwrights with a challenge that would really challenge their creative ability.

People look to television as they would to a Senior member of the family circle.

With best wishes for your new plans,

Yours sincerely,

Mary Whitehouse
(Clean Up TV Campaign)

London Borough of Islington, Town Hall,
Upper Street, London N1
14 November 1966

To: Sydney Newman Head of BBC Drama Television Centre

Dear Mr. Newman,

In yesterday's issue of 'The People' there appeared on page 10 an article headed 'A TV Shocker that will Shame Britain' which refers to a play entitled 'Cathy Comes [sic] Home' due to be shown on BBC television on Wednesday next, the 16th instant.

This article contains a quotation attributed to you including the following remarks:-

'One scene in an Islington tenement, took place in a kitchen that contained the lavatory, 'You can sit on it and do the cooking' is one line from the play, and it is true'.

So far as I know it is Popham Cottages of which it is popularly said, 'You can sit on the lavatory and do the cooking' and if it is a fact that your play 'Cathy Comes Home' has been photographed in Popham Cottages, I should like you and your audiences to know that this Council has bought these dwellings to ensure that they are pulled down as soon as the Families (335 in all) can be rehoused in decent accommodation complying with present day standards. Meantime as any flat becomes vacant, it will not be relet.

Yours faithfully,

C.M.

Associate Town Clerk

Welwyn Garden City, Herts.
Wednesday

Dear Sir,

I wish to protest <u>most strongly</u> about tonight's programme at 9.40 'Up the Junction'. It is pandering to the lowest taste and is <u>positively vulgar</u>. This is dangerous especially when decent minded people are fighting for a moral uplift amongst youngsters.

With venereal diseases on the increase this kind of programme should be scrapped and a better, cleaner way of life shown. One can always pick up dirt without the B.B.C. throwing it in one's face – what a waste of a good medium for finer things.

R.C. (Mrs.)

London W10

3 November 1965

To: Director of Television Programmes, British Broadcasting Corporation, Broadcasting House Portland Place, London W1

Dear Sir,

In today's newspaper I have read to my horror that you intend to 'cut' tonight's production of the television play 'Up the Junction'.

Having greatly enjoyed the book, I found nothing to object to in it and fail to see why all the scenes included in the book should [not] be covered in their entirety in the television adaptation.

I would also be grateful if you would tell me on whose decision these cuts were made, when no objections have been made by the public, as the play has not been screened.

Yours faithfully,

D. J. P.

Aslockton, Notts.

27 February 1963

To: K. Adam, Esq., B.B.C., London

Dear Mr. Adam,

I am not sure which department of the B.B.C. I should write to, but it is always easier to write to somebody one knows rather than to an impersonal body like the B.B.C. hence my letter to you.

Is there no means of effectively protesting about the level of morals and language shown on some of the TV programmes? My wife and I and our two older mid-teenage children were watching your play 'The Prisoner' on Sunday evening. Though it was a grim play in that it appeared to be historically realistic, we considered that it would do the children no harm to watch it. At about 9.30 however, it suddenly descended without warning into the depths of filth and sordidness that I had not seen beaten on TV for some time. The children are not ignorant, and indeed, as the crew-yard of the next-door farm is immediately beside our house and is inhabited largely by pigs, they have only to glance from the windows to see nature in an expanse of mud and filth. By comparison with your play, the view from these windows was a model of purity and cleanliness.

If we want to see a dirty film we can always go to the cinema, but for the B.B.C. suddenly to project dirtiness into one's drawing room without warning ought to be a criminal offence. Your play should have been prefaced by the remark 'This play, in the middle, will suddenly descend into the depths of sordidness and sexual perversion'

Yours sincerely,

D. E. S.

Windlesham, Surrey

16 June 1966

For the personal attention of Hugh [sic] Wheldon B.B.C. London

Dear Mr Wheldon,

My wife and I consider ourselves to be quite broad-minded people and we are certainly not prudes. We consider that the moral standard of the plays shown on BBC Television today have deteriorated to such an extent that they are no longer suitable for viewing by teenaged children or, indeed, their parents. Last night we watched the Wednesday Night play, 'Soiree at Bossom's Hotel'. As usual, it was not only a play of poor standing, but one scene showed two coloured girls performing a most immoral 'strip' dance, which was, to say the least, quite revolting.

The B.B.C. used to be highly respected everywhere but I can assure you that your plays and Satirical programmes give you a very bad name, and I can speak with authority because I talk to people of all nationalities on my world wide travels, who have visited England.

Richard Dimbleby was highly respected all over the world and we certainly miss him and his influence. It would be a splendid achievement if you and your Corporation could emulate his fine example.

Sincerely,

(Capt.) M. C.

Bristol

7 February 1964

To: Kenneth Adam, Director of Programmes, BBC Television

Dear Mr Adam,

My wife and I not only endorse the neurotic, senseless overportrial [sic] of sex, plotlessness and general weirdness accusations which have been made against your Corporation's plays, but we would like to point out that both you and your Producers and Playwrights are indirectly employed by the taxpayer.

The accent on sex to the slowing up of the story and in particular the shots when he trys [sic] to smash a chamber pot with his bare hands, when he asks his wife if he has 'satisfied her' – after getting up from the first sleep with her, and some of the language in the factory scenes were totally unnecessary.

You may query as to why we did not switch off and I would like to say we kept it on because we were fascinated in watching taxpayers money being wasted and wondered if you might decend [sic] to the play's ultimate conclusion i.e. of going even beyond some of the sexual smut you did, in fact show, which would at least have given us the satisfaction of knowing that perhaps some of the people connected with the show might have ended up in Jail.

I only wish other people would similarly protest at the majority treatment given to the extreme minority of people who like pointless, smutty, neurotic and 'Pinter'-like type of Drama.

Sincerely,

D. V. L.

Bristol

14 February 1964

To: Kenneth Adam, Director of Programmes, BBC Television

Dear Mr Adam,

Many thanks for your extremely short reply to my letter of complaint concerning weird, neurotic and rude plays. If you persist in defending 'Trevor' on such flimsy evidence (especially not having seen it) in the face of overwhelming evidence throughout the UK that most viewers deplored it, you will surely make yourself more of a laughing stock than your unfortunate remark in Bristol did, when you excused such type of TV Drama on the grounds that 'they write like that today.'

Personally, throughout the country I don't think even reviewers are other than in a majority against 'Trevor' and (if it's not troubling you too much) I should like to have your comment on the Daily Sketch article attacking the play, which set out the very pompous remarks of the playwright Mr D Turner, who appears to think there is something very wrong with people complaining!!

I have now written to the author of the play along the lines of the first letter I addressed to you, and I have had replies from the two MPs mentioned which suggest that the matter of irresponsibility of yourself, producers and playwrights in the face of taxpayers wishes, will be taken further.

Sincerely

D.V.L.

Bristol

20 February 1964

To: Director of TV BBC cc. Robert Cooke M.P.

Dear Sir,

The 'Festival' Play last night once more demonstrated the BBC's complete lack of appreciation of what the public wants.

It was yet another 'weirdie' type of play and one wonders how people can be expected to believe that such mentally deranged characters exist in such profusion.

Obscenity, bestiality, smut and sex appears to be the current BBC 'bull market', but I doubt, as a whole, if playwrights really have this neurotic kink. Obviously if the BBC create the chamber pot/mental home type of market, a few writers will bury their scruples and continue to churn them out.

I suggest to people who regard this great waste of taxpayers money as a public scandal, that they write to their MP, also the Director of Television B.B.E. [sic] Television Centre London W12.

By-the-way, the title of the play was 'Say Nothing.' It's a pity the author didn't.

D.V. L.

Postman's Piece, The Wold, Claverley, Nr. Wolverhampton

4 February 1965

To: Charles Curran BBC Broadcasting House London W1

Dear Sir,

Thanks for your letter of 27th January. I feel, frankly, that your reply, though most courteous, underlines very much the wide gap which exists between those who produce programmes and those who view them!

Violence such as portrayed in Culloden – particularly the slashing of the face, the bayoneting of the child – was tremendously real (this was supposed to be one of its virtues according to the critics!)

Programmes of this kind bring violence right into the heart of the family circle and not only shock the sensitivities of people but also make it ever more commonplace.

Yours faithfully,

(Mrs.) Mary Whitehouse

Speldhurst, Kent

8 January 1966

My dear Huw [Wheldon],

I hesitate to take advantage of a friendship which goes back to the time when you were still at the L.S.E. but I don't know anyone better to write to on the spiritual education of young people.

We are getting used to unsuitable plays on television but did you see the play called 'The Bone Yard' [written by Clive Exton] on BBC1 on 5th inst? It was about a Police Superintendent who 'took off' the voice of Christ from a Crucifix in a church yard in order to upset the mental balance of one of his own constables in order to give grounds for his dismissal from the force so that the Superintendent could seduce the constable's wife! Apart from what most Christians would regard as blasphemy the plot itself was sufficiently objectionable but together it made my blood boil to think that some of my seventeen grandchildren and thousands of other teenagers would be lapping it up as 'modern culture'.

One could hardly hope that [Director General Hugh] Greene would do anything to stop this sort of 'muck' (there is no other word for it) being broadcast to millions of young and ignorant people but you are so keen on the arts and culture I dare to hope you can use your influence in the position you now hold in the B.B.C.

I remain

Sincerely,

[Mr Illegible!!]

Westbridge, Surrey

5 January 1966

To: The Director of Television, British Broadcasting Corporation, Broadcasting House, London W.1

Sir,

I am speaking for several viewers who saw the 9pm 'The Wednesday Play' called the Boneyard.

We were very shocked as must thousands of other viewers be very shocked by the profane manner in which the Cross was treated together with a most banale [sic] and false characterisation of a senior superior officer of the Police and the portrayal of a constable as a simpleton.

The whole play in which the title of Boneyard for the sacred place where our dear ones lie is in itself a definite insult to the dead and the living, is about the lowest thing that the B.B.C. have descended to and we, amongst thousands of others who must be shocked also, not to speak of the huge criminal class audience [!!!!] who must be very amused at the belittling of the Police by a supposedly responsible organisation, are persuaded that the degrading of morale is the subject of such a play.

The thousands of emigrants leaving England each week for Australia or New Zealand are wise because if the national standards are to be lowered as it would appear to be your object then God help us.

Yours truly,

J. G-G.

Liverpool 18

25 May 1966

To: The Governors B.B.C. London

Dear Sirs,

My wife and I have just seen the Wednesday Play 'Toddler on the Run'. We are quite certain that tonight's play emanated from a twisted mind. We fail to see any merit in it. We know that any number of our friends are switching off their sets after having seen but a small portion of what you, in your colossal ignorance, consider what is fit for our viewing. In our semi-public position, we come into contact with many, many people daily and without exception your image can only be described as evil. You represent a threat to the moral welfare of our children and apart from the news, we should be glad to vote for the abolition of this Country's television services. We know we can always switch you off but we have hoped until now that we would have some return for the licence fee we pay. I know that many other people feel as we do. I only wish they would make their protest.

I accuse you of a complete lack of morality in the selection of your plays, of a total lack of understanding of what ordinary people wish to view.

Only a percentage of our young people, thank God, have become 'Queers' but these are the people you appear to have chosen as the true representatives of the culture of this age. How wrong can you be? Unfortunately, I have paid for my Television licence.

With no apologies, I remain

Completely dissatisfied

B. H.

Corby, Northants.

9 March 1966

Dear Mr. Adam,

On returning home last Wednesday evening my husband and I found our 'teenage' children watching an apparently harmless play dealing with a school war memorial. We joined them but very soon, with no warning, we found ourselves watching rape, gloatingly presented. We were very embarrassed and horrified to have such a scene in our sitting room.

We have tried to bring up our children (and those of others since we are both teachers) with decent Christian standards. I feel that constantly to force upon us scenes of violence and degradation of which the above is only one example, undermines all we strive for.

There must be many thousands of parents, like us, who are deeply disturbed and distressed at what is being brought into our homes. Can you give us no help, no hope? I cannot believe that our concern is unshared.

Yours sincerely,

M.H. (Mrs.)

Aslockton, Notts.

8 November 1965

To: K. Adam, Esq., B.B.C., London

Dear Mr. Adam,

It seems to me that you are in something of a quandary if you are not prepared for the TV to be a mirror. [I]f the TV is to reflect life as it is (this in spite of what you say about using it as a mirror) then there is still [an] obligation on the programme selectors to select which bit of life they reflect. I can, after all, use a mirror to look at a beautiful piece of scenery; I can also use a mirror to look at the bottom of a cesspit. The fact that unpleasant and immoral things take place in contemporary life is well-known, but this does not mean that they are typical or should be selected for entertainment. To select them so frequently (as is done at present) is bound to influence viewers (especially younger ones) to the belief that such scenes not only happen but are normal and acceptable.

The argument, therefore, that the unpleasant scenes happen is no justification whatever for selecting them for TV, it is merely a proof that the TV is a mirror that is being unwisely used.

Yours faithfully,

D. E. S.

Nottingham

4 November 1965

To: Mr Kenneth Adam, BBC, London

Dear Mr Adam,

Last night I read in the Nottingham 'Evening Post' an account of what was described as 'a rumpus' after which you threatened to walk out of a meeting having been heckled by a member of the Nottingham Branch of the Clean Up T.V. Campaign. Tonight, I see from the same paper that the B.B.C. is in trouble again – the cleaner uppers apparently object to the screening last night of a 'pornographic, revolting, smutty' play called 'Up The Junction'. I only wish I had been able to see it since it appears to have been about life as it is lived.

I do not think you are likely to take too much notice of these self-appointed guardians of our purity but it may help a little to know that there are many of us who whole-heartedly approve of programmes with some punch.

I see a few programmes I do not like but you would have to be a miracle worker to please everybody.

Above all, I am sure you would agree, no-one has any <u>right</u> to dictate what someone else should or should not see or hear.

More power to your elbow!

Yours sincerely,

K. W.

CHAPTER SIX

BAD TASTE

One person's bad taste is another person's hilarious comedy or deeply moving drama. The people who find a programme in bad taste tend to write in to complain. The people who do not see a problem do not feel it necessary to write in to let the BBC know that they do not find a particular programme in bad taste. It would therefore be unwise to draw the conclusion from the letters that follow in this section that the BBC was deliberately producing a great many programmes that were in bad taste.

What is possible to see from this section's letters is that it is the traditional subjects of sex and religion above all which produce the most complaints. Churchmen are well represented in this book because they were extremely active in informing the BBC of their displeasure and the likely impact of its bad taste on the morals of their congregants. There was really very little the BBC could do in response.

Fed up with what he perceived as the BBC's inability to control its programme makers and at its support of them in the controversies that followed, our first correspondent in this section takes his complaint to the only person he can imagine who might have the power to tell the BBC to restore the country to the path of moral certainty. His letter is echoed by many in the section entitled That Word as it deals with the famous word uttered by the Literary Manager of the National Theatre on a late-night discussion programme called *BBC-3*, but it is included here because he clearly believes his reader will share his fear for her country's moral welfare.

Budleigh Salterton, Devon
14 November 1965

To: the Queen's Most Excellent Majesty, Buckingham Palace, London SW1

Madam,

Your Majesty is perhaps aware that despite continuous protests from many of your subjects the British Broadcasting Corporation is constantly transmitting highly objectionable pictures, language and ideas to the millions of potential listeners and viewers. A civilised person endeavours, of course, to avoid all contact with such transmissions but this is not always possible and in any case is not the answer to this evil.

Last night, by chance, I saw the programme 'B.B.C.3' for about 3 or 4 minutes. In that short time a revolting idea was discussed by several people, including a 'woman' and a 'man' used a word which even the lowest and most degraded man would hesitate to use even to another man. I will not detail my own feelings of disgust and shame. I am sure they would be shared by Your Majesty who would also feel a righteous anger that such insults should be offered by responsible people to you and all decent people.

An hour or so previously Your Majesty was present at a ceremony in the Royal Albert Hall when the name of Almighty God was invoked and the memories of a million dead were honoured. All such memories and all such honour is insulted by people who deliberately seek to shame and disgrace us.

I implore Your Majesty to use every vestige of authority which you possess to stop this shame and to voice your own condemnation of these people. I assure you that millions of your subjects will whole-heartedly support you. I should like to include your husband and your mother in this supplication.

I beg to remain Your Majesty's loyal subject,
F. S.

Bellewstown, Drogheda
13 November 1960

Dear Sir,

Regarding the Sunday afternoon film 'They Knew What They Wanted' which I have just finished watching – do you honestly consider that a film about an engaged girl who is having a baby by another man is a suitable form of entertainment for Sunday afternoon?

There are so many excellent films which sex does not enter into. And today particularly, being Armistice Sunday, would not one of the many marvellous war films have been more appropriate for both adults and children?

I was only thankful that my 3 children are still too young to watch TV seriously – but what of the thousands of families who have 10–15 year olds at day school and presumably in this cold winter weather spending the afternoon indoors?

P. G.

Blandford Forum, Dorset
15 July 1963

To: Stuart Hood, Director of Programmes, B.B.C. Television

Dear Mr. Hood,

I have never written a letter to the B.B.C., containing adverse comments of one of its programmes, but I am doing so now in respect of the programme 'Sex and Family Life' in your series 'This Nation Tomorrow'.

We live in a free country and expression should be allowed to all but it is surely the duty of the BBC to see that this freedom of expression is not used in an entirely irresponsible way. Dr. Alex Comfort's thesis that sexual intercourse should be considered entirely normal amongst teenagers and that the intrusion of a third person in a relationship should be accepted has surely shocked thousands of ordinary adults. But – and this is my real complaint – it will have inflicted considerable harm on teen-agers as well.

It was regrettable that two of the questioners were to a certain extent supporters of Dr. Comfort and I greatly admired the moral courage of Ruth Robinson, who spoke for many of us, who, in various ways, are trying to help the young people at a difficult and bewildering stage in their lives.

Yours sincerely,

A.T.J.

Penrith Presbyterian Church of England

6 February 1961

To: the Director General BBC Broadcasting House London W1

Dear Sir,

Further to my letter of 20th January forwarding a resolution in connection with the continued lowering of the standard of programme being put on by the B.B.C., [it] was concerned with the general tendency of programmes over the last year or two to include degrading and sordid details, and to deal with promiscuous sexual relationships in an off-hand, matter-of-fact way, which was considered to be degrading and demoralizing.

It may be relevant to state that the Session of this Church includes men of experience and responsibility, including a Doctor, the Chairman of a magistrates' Court, Business men, a Retired Senior Civil Servant and three Senior Police Officers. I mention this to indicate that this resolution has not been passed by an irresponsible body of men but by a group of people of wide experience who are seriously concerned about the effect of this kind of feature on the new generation.

Yours faithfully,

R.M.

Clerk

London W5

11 October 1961

To: Kenneth Adam Esq., Director of Television Broadcasting, Broadcasting House, London W1

Dear Sir,

'TONIGHT' TELEVISION PROGRAMME

On the 3rd October my wife wrote a letter of remonstrance about the sketch in the 'Tonight' programme on the 2nd and she received a duplicated letter addressed to 'Dear Viewer' and carrying the duplicated signature of Miss Kathleen Haacke. Surely, if you had enough complaints to warrant duplicating a reply it might have been very much better for Mr. Michelmore to have offered an apology in the next programme.

Miss Haacke expressed the hope that we would still watch the programme. We have done so, so far, only to be disgusted once again by the representation on 10th October of Noah speaking to God with the cheap familiarity an adolescent might use towards someone for whom he had nothing but contempt, and finally implying criticism of God's behaviour. Both this and the previous example of irreverence would disgrace a group of conceited schoolboys. Coming from supposedly intelligent adults they are utterly nauseating. Moreover, to very many people, my wife and I among them, this kind of thing is blasphemous and causes real distress.

This programme has commanded great respect in the past and this latest trend is quite beneath the producers and the cast. I suggest it would be better for them to close down before damaging the goodwill they have build up both for themselves and for the Corporation.

Yours faithfully,

M.S.

Chartered Architect & Surveyor

London W5
26 October 1961

To: Kenneth Adam Esq., Director of Television Broadcasting, Broadcasting House, London W1

Dear Mr. Adam,

Many thanks for your friendly letter of the 20th.

All you say is perfectly reasonable and, now that the heat of the moment is passed, I agree that the Andre Obey adaptation did not overstep accepted standards of decency. Neither the original piece nor the adaptation are in any way remarkable against the general background of the literature and drama of our time and I agree that their production does not necessarily show intentional irreverence or bad taste. My wife and I and very many other people find this state of affairs very disturbing indeed.

I am quite sure that humour and a sense of fun is a good thing in all our activities including religion but I am equally certain that flippancy directed towards the Bible is utterly incompatible with reverence towards God. The increasingly widespread acceptance of this kind of thing as good entertainment and the freedom with which entertainers supply it are distressing to many people. I am sure that no-one could be better aware than yourself of the effect that such bodies as the BBC have on the formation of public opinion and even the thinking of individuals.

I know that you do take your responsibilities very seriously indeed and I hope you will not think me impertinent in saying I only wish you could see this matter as my wife and I do.

Yours sincerely,

M.S.

Chartered Architect & Surveyor

Waterloo, Liverpool 22
2 October 1961

To: The Director General, B.B.C., London

Sir,

I beg to refer to the last but one item on the 'TONIGHT' programme of Monday 2nd October in which there was a caricature of two ordained priests of the Church of England standing on a lectern and reading in the language of the Bible some stupid silly diatribe which I gathered was intended to be a skit on advertising.

I am appalled and disgusted that your programme department should engage in, what to me is such depravity and sacrilege.

As a practising member of the Church of England I protest most strongly and shall be glad to know that steps are taken to cease such sordid exhibitions.

I and many others feel strongly about this lack of good taste. May I solicit the favour of your early reply, please? Yours faithfully,

S.K.W.

Fareham, Hants
20 October 1962

To: the BBC London

Sir,

It is with great regret that in spite of our correspondence [of last month] in connection with [the drama] Stamboul Train, I find it necessary to draw attention to another slip of good taste.

This evening, Oct 20th, at about 7.47–7.49pm you were showing a young man who appeared to be a Pop singer walking to a bar in a club that was empty except for the bar tender. His words mentioned this as he began to croon. The barman then offered him a drink as he seated himself on a tall stool. He raised the glass: tossed the drink down his throat: and then in a brassy manner half spat, half dribbled the liquid down over his chin as though this was a most respectable and socially acceptable way in which to behave.

The detail that was objectionable was the slobbering.

All the viewers who may not have been trained to proper ways of handling their drinks have absorbed the unconscious suggestion that it is proper for an artist of good repute to be seen behaving in this manner. It is now quite inevitable that some of the younger viewers will have gained the notion that that is a fine way to behave.

This is highly disturbing and it seems that your methods of vetting productions stands in need of serious overhaul.

Yours sincerely,

(Rev.) G.C.N.

Copy to Cardiff Education Authority

Romiley, Cheshire

10 November 1963

To: The Director General, The British Broadcasting Corporation

Dear Sir,

As members of the Catholic 'Look Listen' Movement representing Catholics throughout Lancashire, we are gravely disturbed by a situation existing at the present time [that] compels us to state our grievance in the form of a protest, viz:

We protest to the British Broadcasting Corporation that it is violating its charter by permitting the broadcasting of material on Radio and TV which is offensive by reason of its being:

a. immoral; e.g. sex 'jokes' (these are an insult to God and an offense to family life) and the morbid highlighting of unsavoury news items

b. irreligious; e.g. the guying of religious institutions and persons

c. anti-social; e.g. the ridiculing of heads of state and persons in authority. The BBC is bound by charter to uphold authority.

We see this departure from the fit standards laid down for the BBC by charter as originating in the TV programme billed as 'That was the week, that was' and gradually spreading to other programmes.

We conceive this lapse to be the fault of an irresponsible minority of BBC Governors, Directors and Producers and call upon their colleagues to repudiate it. We consider the BBC 'air' belongs to the community and not the entertainment industry and that there is no room in it for 'dirty' night club entertainment.

The BBC belongs to us and our families, and even as a minority we have a right to demand that it should not harm them. We believe also that we speak for many others who know of no way to make their views known. We have chosen this way. If it is unsuccessful we shall have to find other methods.

Yours faithfully,

M.D.S.

North West Look Listen Committee

Bournemouth

21 May 1964

To: Hugh Greene Esq., Broadcasting House, London W1

Dear Sir,

Referring to your letter of the 27th ult. Those [plays] that I have seen I have endeavoured to forget; but the same low moral attitude of mind is also seeping into and permeating even the children's programmes.

It was said by the reader of the letters, deputising for Robert Robinson, in Junior Points of View. A little girl, aged five, had evidently been viewing parts of Lorna Doone and had enjoyed seeing the cattle in one of the country scenes. She concluded her letter by writing 'and now we have a cow called Lorna'. The reply to this was, 'It's interesting to know because I have a bull called Doone. We must see that they are put together.' There was not the slightest justification on any count for such a remark.

I recall another instance of a quite unnecessarily degrading presentation, viz: The Beggars Opera. I remember Sir Nigel Playfair's production, this was delightful entertainment. The B.B.C. production was lewd, bawdy and ugly; one couldn't enjoy even the good singing.

May I suggest that the principles laid down by the first Governor of the B.B.C. that 'the people, inclining their ear to whatsoever things are honest, beautiful and of good report may tread the path of wisdom and righteousness.' At one time the B.B.C. obeyed these principles and won the admiration and

respect of the listening world. There has been for a long time
a subtle but determined intention on the part of foreigners to
belittle, degrade, humiliate and even ridicule Britain. The B.B.C.
can lift its head and stand firm by its original principles.

There is one other defect – poor and loose enunciation mostly
on the part of women announcers. There is not one on BBC1 who
knows how to speak clearly.

Yours faithfully,

D.W.L. (Miss)

The Mothers' Union Westminster SW1

22 September 1964

**To: K. Adam Esq. C.B.E. B.B.C. Television Centre, Wood
Lane, London W12**

Dear Mr. Adam,

I am writing on behalf of the Central Watch and Social
Problems Committee of the Mothers' Union to ask whether
you have a programme in mind on the <u>moral</u> issue of venereal
disease.

The programme on Monday, September 7th at 9.45pm
was extremely interesting but it was clearly stated that it was
concerned only with the medical side, and my Committee felt that
a programme on the moral issues involved would be immensely
valuable and would make a greater impact on television than
on radio.

Yours sincerely,

Mrs. R.P.

CHAPTER SEVEN

RADIO SWEARING

Although the majority of letters in this book concern television programmes, the files in the BBC's Written Archive date back to the start of the wireless service. People got just as exercised about things they didn't like on the radio as they were later to do about television. Consistently, it appears that they objected vociferously to what they called swearing. Some of the words they objected to will certainly come as a surprise to present day readers, but then they would probably have come as a bit of a surprise to the outraged correspondents in the 1960s as well, which just goes to prove that each era interprets what it regards as offensive or obscene in its own way. The correspondents who believed radio and television unleashed a torrent of vile words into their living rooms would presumably have thought it faintly ridiculous that Victorians would cover up the legs of teir dining room tables for fear of arousing lustful feelings.

Since 1945 there has been an unmistakable coarsening of the English language in everyday speech. Words which would then have been largely the province of male only environments are now to be heard in public, read in novels and seen in profusion on the internet, spoken and written by both genders. The words to which the correspondents took exception in the 1960s, to say nothing of the 1940s, have lost their power to shock but what follows is a series of letters from an earlier time when such words were regarded with the utmost seriousness. One has only to think of the trouble David Selznick had in persuading the Hays Office in 1939 to let him use the notorious last line of Margaret Mitchell's novel *Gone with the Wind*. It would be as well to bear this mind when reading what looks to us to be an absurd over-reaction to what was heard on the wireless.

Egham, Surrey
13 December 1943

To: The Director, B.B.C.

Dear Sir,

I protest with all vigour against the language put over the air in the play 'They went singing' of yesterday afternoon. A former objection of mine was ignored and I presume went into the w.p.b. as a letter from a crank. Coming in from Sunday School my ears were assailed with 'bloodys', 'damns', 'what the hell', 'blasts' and God's holy name being used in a most irreverent manner.

If an author or producer cannot make a play really alive without using objectionable words they can scarcely be worth the expense of the B.B.C. engaging them – a decent minded, clean thinking author if he has any real ability can beget vitality without this language. Proper minded women and innocent children ought not to have the unloveliness [sic] of men's adjectives polluting their ears and minds.

Why not go the whole hog and allow 'funny' men of the stage [to] tell their smutty stories and filthy suggestions over the air – there will always be plenty who enjoy jokes and language that savour of the cesspool. 'Keep it clean' is now a stock joke but the times badly need clean thinking, clean talking and clean living. What with this kind of stuff and with the infernal din of jazz-bands, the mawkish sentimentality of crooners and the distressing noises of 'harmonists' and swing music one hesitates to switch on the wireless at all.

I am, Sir, yours very truly,

(Rev.) A.C.T.

Ashtead, Surrey
23 March 1944

To: The Director of Religious Broadcasting, B.B.C. London

Dear Sir,

I wish to protest most strongly against the increasing use of the expression 'Oh Lord' by juvenile characters in Children's Hour (e.g. 'Moonlight Castle' today). We have unfortunately become used to the taking of God's name in vain in the general programmes, but quite apart from the disregard of the third commandment and the contempt which generally follows undue familiarity with the Holy Name, the effect on a young mind must be most perplexing when prayers follow which commence with the same expression!

Will you in the interests of the rising generation please see that this letter reaches the quarter controlling Children's Hour and will you add your protest?

Yours truly,

R.S.

London
17 April 1944

To: The Director General, B.B.C.

Dear Sir,

Desert Highway by J.B. Priestley

I wish to express my profound disapproval of the amount of common swearing as broadcast in the above on Saturday night 15th inst.

As the guardian of public morals and the potential champion of cultural 'uplift' I consider the Corporation has in this case signally failed, and has done a serious disservice to the community.

Yours faithfully,

F. A. S.

Guildford, Surrey
23rd May 1945

Sir,

Where are the B.B.C.'s censors? We do not care for the language that was inflicted on us on Tuesday night in 'The Battle of Britain'. Don't retort, 'You need not listen if you don't want to'. We did not know it was coming. It was bawled out with nearly enough violence to wreck the loud speaker. We switched off immediately fearing the depths of profanity to which the feature might sink as the excitement increased.

All decent minded people find coarse language offensive, and Christians object most strenuously to the blasphemous use of the name of Jesus Christ.

I remain,

Yours faithfully,

(Mrs.) R.E.S.

Dewsbury, Yorkshire
22 May 1945

To: The Religious Director B.B.C.

My dear Sir,

I am not easily shocked having been in the last war and being one of your contemporaries at Knutsford: but I have just listened to the broadcast 'Now it can be told' – a most interesting talk but entirely spoiled for me by a blasphemous quotation half way through. The speaker quoted a New Zealand pilot and the words used began with the expression, 'Christ Almighty' and included the not very desirable word 'bloody'. It was the kind of broadcast that would attract a large number of children listeners and I think you will agree that the work of a parish priest in his instructions is going to be demolished if this kind of thing is permitted. I am wondering whether the script was submitted for inspection and, if it was, what is the attitude of the B.B.C. towards this usage?

I would be glad if you would use your influence in this matter if you are unable to take the matter up let me know to whom to write. The matter should not be allowed to pass without protest otherwise both of us had better shut up shop.

Yours faithfully,

G. S.

[P.S.] The broadcast would have lost nothing of its effectiveness had the objectionable words been excluded.

Debenham, Suffolk
15 November 1945

Dear Sir,

I was really disgusted at the swear words used in the play on Monday evening @ 8 o'clock.

We are trying to plan a better world. Can we do so where the young listen to such words as 'Damn' and 'Blast'? These words were frequently used in the play. I know of families who will not have the wireless in their homes because of the children.

I am a widow, having lost a young son, an officer. My late husband was a schoolmaster also a Justice of the Peace.

I sincerely hope and pray that the wireless create[s] a higher atmosphere.

Yours faithfully,

K. P.

Moss Side, Manchester
Saturday night May 1946

Dear Sir,

Why do you allow those actors and actresses to blaspheme God's name? The play has only just begun and they have used God's name already half a dozen times.

Well, I have just had to turn it off. I daren't listen any longer and sometimes I enjoy the Saturday play.

Do you realise that allowing people to broadcast who blaspheme even if it is only a play is enough to keep the world in the state it is in to-day and worse, yes and even to cause atom bombs to be used and the world destroyed.

It doesn't make the play or the acting more effective, it spoils it right away and lowers it and especially when it is never said in our homes.

Then the young ones hear it and a lot of them don't go to Sunday School so they will get used to it. The responsibility rests on you. Do not allow it for their sake and yours and also for the world at large.

Yours sincerely,

E. S.

P.S. You might think that it doesn't matter, that it is only a small thing, that there are worse things going on in the world, but every little wrong counts and would rebound again, arousing more and more troubles and haven't we had enough? I think of those who have died that we might live. At any rate you can stop that and that will be one wrong put right.

College Place, Southampton

17 January 1947

To: The B.B.C. London

Dear Sirs,

<u>Re Childrens Hour.</u>

The final words in the Children [sic] Hour last evening consisted of, be damned to it.

Will you please justify such language, words of this description are never heard in many houses, one of which is mine, and I very strongly resent this being brought in via the wireless.

Re other Programmes, may I also point out to you that if similar language to that used in some of the other programmes was used in certain Public Places the Police if present would have to take action.

Yours faithfully,

E.S.P.

Drapers, Tailors & Outfitters

Sheffield 3
2 November 1947

To: The Director of Plays etc. B.B.C.
Dear Sir,

A word of congratulation on the 'Plays and Dramas' you are giving to us, and the very fine themes contained in most of them but this is not the principal reason of this letter. My object is to strongly protest against such good plays etc. being completely ruined by the foul and offensive language which is used in some of them and the very limit being reached on October 24th at 9-15pm in the 'Home Service', when 'After All' was being given. I arrived home after this play had commenced, but quickly picked up the theme only to have the whole thing spoiled by the very offensive language used at the 'climax' of the Play.

As a Layman of the Methodist Church and a Leader of Young People, and incidentally an advocate of them listening to these plays I trust my protest may be the means of obliterating this offensive language, and our young people listening only to the very best of language.

Thanking you in anticipation.

Yours Sincerely,

G. P.

Goole, Yorkshire
6 December 1947

**To: The Director of Dramatic Programmes, The B.B.C.
London**
Dear Sir,

On Saturday night I turned on the Home Service Programme two or three times between 9/45 and 10/45pm, and on each occasion I was greeted with a torrent of blasphemy, damnation and bad language that offended my ears.

On looking at the programme given in my newspaper, I find the production was called 'Touchwood', and I assume it was either a play or a story. I shall be much obliged if you will inform me whether it comes under the heading of 'Culture' or 'Amusement'. If the former it should possess some edifying qualities, and I shall be glad to know what these are, and the type of mind that is supposed to benefit from them. If the latter, there is always a class that seems to enjoy any turgid stream of sex and profanity that is poured out, but surely the bulk of your listeners are not of this type and is it necessary to lower the standard of broadcasting to satisfy the craving of this class of the community?

I am,

Yours faithfully,

W. H. W.

Forest of Dean Miners' Association

17 February 1932

To: Sir John Reith

Dear Sir,

I am quite sure that many listeners were deeply offended by the derogatory expression made about the Right Hon. Mr. D. Lloyd George on Monday night by one of the Vaudeville Artists.

Mr. Lloyd George was described as a 'Welsher'. As you know, this terms refers to bookmakers who run away from a racecourse without settling or paying their bets.

I wish to protest against the use of the microphone to libel anyone, whoever he is.

I would point out that Mr. Herbert Smith, former president of the Miners' Federation of Great Britain, was sued for using the same expression and was made to pay £2000 damages.

I am writing the B.B.C. and Mr. Lloyd George also.

Yours faithfully,

J. W.

CHAPTER EIGHT

RADIO SATIRE

The common belief is that political satire began on the BBC in November 1962 with the first broadcast of *That Was the Week That Was*. In fact, it is possible to find letters complaining about the political bias of the BBC in its comedy programmes dating back to the 1940s.

Given the landslide result of the 1945 general election in which Labour was returned to power with 393 seats compared to the Conservatives' 197, it appeared that the country was firmly behind the new administration. The post-war Labour government might have been elected in a summer of peace and amidst deep and widespread hope for the future, but Britain had emerged from World War II with its economy almost in ruins. Initially, at least, it was determined to keep hold of the Empire but the economic implications of its upkeep and the political reality of the growth of nationalism soon made that impossible.

Meanwhile there were shortages and rationing, a devaluation of sterling, a desperate export drive, demobbed men struggling to fit back into their family lives after six years of total war and, in 1946–7, one of the worst winters that ever blighted this island. The problem here was that there was not enough fuel and the population just froze. Any government facing such social, economic and political turmoil would soon find itself beleaguered as the Socialist Utopia failed to materialise.

As it was in so many cases, the BBC found itself in the firing line even though it frequently went to enormous lengths to remain politically impartial. In 1949, Ealing Studios made a very funny and pointed film about life under the post-war Labour government called *Passport to Pimlico*, which imagined what life in one district of south west London might be like devoid of the petty regulations that so afflicted the everyday lives of the British population, but it seems unlikely that Michael Balcon, the executive in charge of production there, would have been subject to the complaints that arrived in a steady stream at Broadcasting House. People who find offence in their own living rooms are much more likely to take up the cudgels than people who go to the cinema or read books.

Compared to what we remember of *Spitting Image*, Harry Enfield and Ben Elton, the comic barbs aimed at the Labour government in the late 1940s were fired with a pop gun but they were sufficient to get a number of Labour supporters very worked up indeed. One of them, writing from Stanmore in Middlesex, was understandably cross about a joke that was broadcast when the polls were still open. It was from the man who was, within days, to become the new prime minister.

Stanmore, Middlesex

14 July 1945

To: The Director, British Broadcasting Corporation

Dear Mr. Hailey,

I have had a letter drawing my attention to a B.B.C. item on Sunday last, July 8th. It stated that Richard Murdoch, in Will Fyffe's programme at 2 o'clock, sang words to the effect 'If we change to Attlee, we might lose the Japanese war'.

This would appear to me to be inexcusable, considering that the Election was still being contested in the 24 Northern constituencies, and I shall be obliged if you will enquire into the matter, and let me have your observations.

Yours sincerely,

C.R. Attlee

St. Pancras Labour Party

25 April 1946

To: The Director General, B.B.C., Portland Place, W.1

Dear Sir,

I was surprised on tuning in at 12.55pm today to discover two comedians in 'Workers' Playtime' singing a song of which the gist was the following:- 'I want to be a refugee from England, that little piece of land where I am not free.' There was another passage suggesting that they in common with most people are 'overtaxed and underfed' and an even more surprising couplet stating that 'If they cannot run England without Churchill they will have to do without me.'

There have been a number of instances recently of subtle anti-Labour and pro-Conservative propaganda, particularly in the alleged funny series of B.B.C. programmes, but so far nothing quite so blatant as this.

I should be glad if you would let me know what action, if any, you propose to take on this matter.

Yours faithfully,

E. C.

Monmouth

7 April 1946

To: Peter Freeman Esq., M.P., House of Commons

Dear Sir,

I should like to call your attention to what, in my humble opinion, is cheap propaganda against the Labour Government, put over the air in a very subtle way. I am referring to the broadcast of two comics. The last turn in Music Hall on Saturday night Apl. 6th. This sort of thing has been going on for a long time. Radio comics are allowed to crack cheap jokes at the expense of the Government and to insult the feeling of thousands who [are] suffering through the conditions in which we find a large number of people today.

I wonder if the [Conservative] opposition had been in power, would they allow it to go on unchecked?

We hear very little reference to the opposition, in broadcasts of this kind, by cheap so-called radio comics. To put it mildly, it is damned rotten, that this sort of propaganda should be allowed to be used against the men who represent the Labour Party, who have the unthankful job of squaring up the biggest mess the country has seen.

Yours faithfully,

S.H.C.

Member Newport No.1 Branch N.U.R. [National Union of Railwaymen]

Prince of Wales Road, Sheffield 2, Yorks.
5 October 1946

Dear Sir,

It is the first time I have ever written to you, but I cannot let last Friday Evening's broadcast by Nosmo King pass without a very strong protest. This comedian ? [sic] could do nothing but pass adverse comments about M.P.s, chiefly the Labour Government. There has been far too much of this lately and I consider it a gross insult to the many thousands who voted for the present Government. This kind of wit did not appear when the Tories were in power.

I always understood that the B.B.C. were Non political but apparently I must have been mistaken.

Yours Truly,

H. P.

Watford, Herts
27 December 1946

Dear Sir,

I wish to draw your attention to a flagrant violation by the B.B.C. of their supposedly non political bias in their broadcast.

The script of 'Heres How' Broadcast [sic] at 10.15p.m. in the Home Service on the 27inst. contained a song purely without entertainment value, and designed to incite the listener against the present government.

While I cannot give you the full words, I have no doubt that the following excerpt will interest you, and I trust that you will be able to take some action in this matter.

'Isn't it a pity that Britons can take it
Isn't it a pity they don't make a fuss
Take the standing in the queues
The failure to house them
That ought to arouse them
As long as they take it without a shout
There are governments that will dish it out.'

While of course this is not the whole song and one or two of my words may vary from the correct ones, I hope that you will consider whether this matter is worthy of further investigation.

I shall take the earliest opportunity of raising this matter at my T.U. branch meeting and at the next meeting of Watford L.P. [Labour Party] to which I have the honour to be this year's A.E.U. [Amalgamated Engineering Union] delegate.

Yours faithfully,

(Sgd.)
A.W.H.

Stoke on Trent
20 September 1947

To: The Programme Director, B.B.C., London, W
Dear Sir,

I would be the last to throw 'brickbats' at the B.B.C. for I think its programmes second to none, and realize that good humoured jokes of topical interest are perhaps more than ever welcome in times of austerity, but at the same time I should like to register a protest at the constant repetition of 'jokes', some of them so stale

too, at the expense of particular members of the Government.
I refer in particular to Stuart MacPherson and the gentleman
introducing 'Up and Doing'.

Some how they seem to be meant to be taken seriously,
whereas one can laugh with some artists at [Minister of Fuel and
Power] Mr. Shinwell, but having seen some of the grim realities
and ugliness of mining districts such as this, it is not always easy
to do that.

Politicians are not sensitive I believe but I am sure many
listeners are.

Yours faithfully,

L.J.S.

Preston, Lancs.

9 October 1948

**To: The Director-General, British Broadcasting
Corporation, London W1**

Sir,

It is only on rare occasions that I listen to the radio feature
'Music-Hall'; and this is the first occasion on which I have
written a letter of this kind to the B.B.C. I desire, however to call
your attention to a 'joke' made by the Western Brothers in their
broadcast this evening.

'Three applicants are up for interview for a big job on the Coal
Board. Each, on being admitted, is asked what twelve twelves
make. Two give the correct answer, one a not very obvious
answer. Then comes the 'joke': Who got the job? The witty
answer was 'Mr. Gaitskell's nephew'.

Now, sir, it seems to me that this sort of thing is in extremely
bad taste. Whether it leaves the perpetrators open to action
for libel I cannot say. Of course I may have a deficient sense of
humour, or there may be some subtlety of humour that I am
unable to perceive. I am aware that this government has been
especially subject to this kind of oblique attack; though most
ministers are not thin-skinned and it is, within reason, salutary

that we should make light of the exigencies of the time. I do not think that one's own particular political views need affect one's judgement, however, as to what is or is not in good taste. I am quite convinced that the incident calls for a public apology. And I shall be surprised if other fair-minded people do not think the same.

I am, Sir,

Yours faithfully,

L.A.R.

London EC2

24 March 1948

To: Miss K. Haacke, The British Broadcasting Corporation, W1

Dear Madam,

It may well be that when I wrote to you about [comic actor] Jack Hulbert's broadcast I did so rather too quickly after hearing it, and had I waited it is more than likely that I should not have written it at all.

I entirely understand that a Government or public men who cannot stand the jests of the comedians have no right to be in the position they are. What did annoy me was that so few people seem to realise the gravity of the country's position and until they do there is no great hope of an improvement in our affairs. The broadcast on the White Paper seemed to me to be the first really firm statement this Government has issued and it seemed a pity to detract from it by laughing at it immediately afterwards.

Do believe that I am all for the B.B.C's policy of avoiding censorship of the comedians. In these circumstances I do feel that the comedian in question, whom I used to know personally and like immensley [sic], did rather overstep the bounds of good taste. I fully realise, however, that the B.B.C. cannot avoid such things and once more I do appreciate your courteous letter.

Yours faithfully,

W.D.W.

CHAPTER NINE

THAT WAS THE WEEK THAT WAS

The largest numbers of files in the Written Archive holding correspondence relating to a specific programme are devoted to *That Was the Week That Was*, or *TW3* as it became known. The second largest is probably those files collected by its successor, *Not So Much a Programme, More a Way of Life*, which is probably on a par with *BBC-3*, the final programme in producer/director Ned Sherrin's trilogy of programmes tarred with the brush of satire.

Sherrin was an Oxford graduate who learned the trade of television production during the mid to late 1950s whilst working on live shows for ATV, the franchise holder for the Midlands area on weekdays. He then moved down to London where he joined the staff of the nightly magazine programme *Tonight*, whose success lay in the way it treated the news entertainingly and slightly irreverently, which was entirely original in the late 1950s. After he had proved his credentials on *Tonight*, Sherrin was charged with the task of finding a British equivalent of the late-night talk show which American television had developed with great success.

Having assembled the cast who were all to become famous very quickly, Sherrin produced and directed two pilot shows, both of which were deeply disliked by his bosses. In subsequent years, Sherrin told two conflicting stories about how *TW3* got the green light to proceed to production. One of them concerned a group of Tory ladies who had been interviewed by Bernard Levin and who were incensed that their appearances had not been seen by the nation. The other, rather more likely version, was that ITV announced it was planning a satire programme of its own.

Sherrin made a virtue of the necessity created by live performance and inadequate rehearsal time and decided to include shots of the studio, the audience, the actors reading their lines off a script and, innovatively, the cameramen going about their work. On Saturday 24 November 1962, Millicent Martin, looked directly into the lens and sang the lyrics of a complicated song she had been given only a few hours before.

> That was the week that was
> It's over let it go
> But what a week it was –
> At Brussels, Ted Heath has the world at his feet
> He got tariff reductions on kangaroo meat,
> Sir Keith Joseph's lady gave the homeless a break
> They called to protest, she said, 'Let 'em eat cake!'

By the time the show meandered to a finish after midnight, the BBC, rather to its own surprise, found that it had commissioned a social revolution.

The BBC's written policy as published in the *BBC Variety Programmes Policy Guide for Writers and Producers* had been to exclude jokes concerned with the following subjects:

> Lavatories
> Effeminacy in men
> Immorality of any kind
> Suggestive references to:
>> Honeymoon couples
>> Chambermaids
>> Fig leaves
>> Prostitution
>> Ladies' underwear e.g. winter draws on

Animal habits e.g. rabbits

Commercial travellers

Interestingly, the BBC refused to be cowed by political pressure and continued to approve jokes about politicians except for 'anything that could be construed as personal abuse of Ministers, Party Leaders or MPs and anything that can reasonably be construed as derogatory to political institutions'. This was the area in which *TW3* was to have a permanent influence and as long as Sherrin, Frost and the writers were protected by Hugh Greene's 'hands off' approach, they were safe to have a go at any politician and any political institution.

Peter Cook had already mercilessly lampooned Macmillan in *Beyond the Fringe*, and *Private Eye* was on the shelves before *TW3* started its remorseless attacks, particularly on the Conservative government of the day, but it was the reach and power of television that made *TW3* so influential. The shrieks that greeted what would now be regarded as relatively gentle satire reveals a population that was astonished, outraged and occasionally thrilled to be confronted in their own living rooms by incontrovertible evidence that the age of deference was dead.

The men who had apparently killed it were Ned Sherrin, a 31-year-old supporter of Somerset County Cricket Club and self-confessed Tory voter, and David Frost, the 23-year-old son of a Methodist minister. To most viewers of the younger generation, *TW3* was a breath of fresh air and the first time they had seen their views about the society in which they lived expressed openly on television. To the vast majority of the letter writers, these men were the Devil Incarnate. Once again, the generation gap that permeated the decade was only too apparent.

Edinburgh

10 December 1962

To: The Director of Television Broadcasting, London W1

Dear Sir,

Saturday's performance of 'That was the Week That was' included an allusion to an alleged appearance of the Virgin Mary.

It was made in a manner, and in association with a quotation from the 'News of the World', that left no reasonable doubt the intention was to hold up the question of any such appearance as a matter for derision and ridicule.

An earlier item in the same programme was the song 'A Rivederci [sic], Roma' by a group of performers garbed as prelates, against a background of St. Peter's. The effect was simply, in default of wit or satire, to present the bishops of the Roman Church as intrinsically subjects for mockery.

I need hardly remind you that it has for long been the policy of the Corporation that seriously controversial items should be broadcast only where 'the material is of high quality'. That condition is hardly satisfied in this programme, featuring a sketch about the half-open (latterly fully open) fly of a man's trousers, suggestive of the sort of thing that might be performed extempore by the personnel of a fourth-rate night-club whose stripper had failed to turn up.

I do not really have very strong feelings about the representation of cardinals doing the twist but it would be agreeable to be assured that the invocation of the Virgin Mary as a character in low comedy is unlikely to be repeated in your programmes.

Yours faithfully,

(Mrs.) A.M.A. B.

Catholic Parents & Electors Association Croydon
12 December 1962

To: The British Broadcasting Corporation, London
Dear Sirs,

I am directed to write to you with regard to 'That Was The Week That Was' [by] my Committee, the elected lay-representatives of parishioners of one of the largest Catholic Parishes in South London.

We have come to the conclusion that the programme's attempt to belittle Religion with a set at the Catholic Faith or as you prefer to call it, the Church of Rome. The jazzing-up of a hymn in last week's programme was in very bad taste, so also was the portrayal of a band of Cardinals taking temporary leave of the Ecumenical Council in Rome.

In the last two productions a reference has been made to the Mass which is the Keystone of our Religion and something therefore that is most sacred to all of us. We have also noted with regret the reference in last Saturday's production to the blessed Virgin Mary: surely She, as the Mother of God, could be spared the ignominy of reference in a satirical revue.

May we please have your assurance that future productions will omit entirely any reference to religious matters. We also hope that songs of such a nature as, 'Bed before Marriage' and subjects of such discussions as a man's fly buttons may no longer have any place in these productions.

Yours faithfully,

D.V.

Lambeth Palace, SE1

18 December 1962

To: Harman Grisewood, Esq., C.B.E., The British Broadcasting Corporation, Broadcasting House, London, W1

Dear Grisewood,

Thank you very much for your letter of 14th December.

Complaints have been made to the Archbishop [of Canterbury] about the following matters in 'That Was The Week That Was'.

1. That on 1st December something to the following effect was said and greeted with sardonic laughter – 'We want to produce a series of three religious epics based on the Creation, Crucifixion and the Resurrection entitled 'God', 'Son of 'God' and 'Return of the Son of God''.

2. That in the programme on 7th December [probably 8th] there was a parody of 'O, God Our Help in Ages Past' and a cheap reference to the Virgin Mary.

3. That on 15th December there was sardonic laughter when Our Lord's words were quoted in relation to a recent appeal for religion in the training of the Army.

I do not comment in any way upon these allegations because neither the Archbishop nor I heard the programmes. This is of course why I ventured to bother you. If you have any way of letting me know exactly what was said at the points referred to in the three programmes it might be very helpful. I am sure you will do what you can.

Yours sincerely,

R. B.

Oxford & Cambridge Club, Pall Mall, SW1

10 December 1962

To: Hugh Carleton Greene, Director, B.B.C.

Dear Hugh,

THAT WAS THE WEEK THAT WAS

I felt I must write to you to say that this T.V. programme is absolutely excellent.

I am a lifelong R.C. and no sensible Catholic could object to the Roman song about the Cardinals. People who cannot take being laughed at are using the mistaken idea that British Catholics are offended by this song as an excuse for trying to get the programme off the air.

I am sure that it is extremely good for this country to lampoon our rulers and institutions, and what is so admirable about the programme is that it is really funny and light hearted and superbly good entertainment value.

For the sake of all our generation at Merton [College, Oxford] do try to keep this programme going as long as possible. To me it is one of the best things I have seen on T.V.

With best wishes,

R. L.

Bognor Regis, Sussex

12 January 1963

To: The Programme Director,
The B.B.C. LONDON

Dear Sir,

I wish to protest most strongly against the blasphemous sketch in the Christian Faith and its Founder, The Lord Jesus Christ, as seen on this Saturday's programme 'This was the week that was'.

My whole family, which does not consist entirely of committed Christians, were horrified at the vulgar and foul way in which this particular sketch was played.

It is particularly disgraceful that the people who have the power to influence the minds and lives of thousands of people show such terrible things, not only blaspheming the name of God, but condemning themselves in the process, and also corrupting that which is designed to build men up, bringing them the peace and hope that millions are seeking for today.

I desire an answer to this letter, hoping that I may have an official assurance that such a sketch may NEVER be allowed on the screens of BBC Television again, IN ANY DEGREE.

I am not ashamed of the strong tone of this letter for I believe the matter to be so vitally important that it needs your immediate attention.

Yours faithfully,

P.J.S.C.

The Tavistock Institute of Human Relations,

3 Devonshire Street, London W1

15 January 1963

To: Kenneth Adam Esq., Director of Television,
TV Centre, Wood Lane, London W12

My dear Kenneth,

I am sure you have had lots of messages about TWTWTW. I only hope that the proportion of complimentary ones is greater than that of the abusive ones.

I thought you would like to know that it is now the habit in teen-age parties held in Blackheath on Saturday night, to suspend all activities during this programme while everyone adjourns to the television set. This, at least, is a unique record – and quite seriously, I think, an important indicator.

Yrs

A.K.R.

The High Commissioner, Republic of Cyprus

5 February 1963

To: Hugh Carleton Greene, Director General, British Broadcasting Corporation, Portland Place, London W1

Sir,

I have been painfully surprised by last Saturday's B.B.C. programme 'That Was The Week That Was' in which reference was made to Archbishop Makarios. This reference to the name of a person with dual capacity as Head of an Independent State and Head of the Autocephalous Church of Cyprus was, to say the least, a most unfortunate one.

What the B.B.C. has done was, in the opinion of all right-thinking people, a gross violation of internationally accepted ethics of morality and respect which are always extended to foreign Heads of State and is deplorable. But is even more deplorable in the case of Archbishop Makarios who is not only the Head of a Commonwealth State but is, at the same time, the Head of the Cyprus Church.

In protesting most vigorously against this lack of courtesy shown to the President of the Cyprus Republic I would like to assure you, Sir, that programmes of this sort do not help to strengthen the good relations which so happily now exist between our two countries.

I have the honour to be, Sir,

Yours faithfully,

High Commissioner

Sanderstead, Surrey

14 April 1963

To: The Governors, B.B.C. Television Service

Dear Sirs,

I wish to confirm my verbal protest given over the telephone to the duty officer about 10.30pm last night, when I informed him of my horror on hearing the blasphemous skit just portrayed by David Frost in 'T.W.T.W.T.W.' The words he spoke were conveyed in the pseudo serious nature of a religious narration and repeated the words of Sacred Scripture but in the place of Christ referred to Chief Enaharo and how the Elders consulted to do him to death. This is most distasteful to the Christian morals of this country. It is the worst episode I have witnessed in this weekly show of bad taste and complete disregard of moral principles. It is, furthermore, an inexcusable ridicule of Sacred Scripture and as such subject to the laws of this Christian Country which still permits legal action to be taken against the perpetrators of blasphemy. Is legal action through the courts necessary in order to make the B.B.C. realise that the Corporation is subject to the Christian morals of this country?

As to the episode on Saturday, will you state in clear terms that you apologise to the listening public for the offence occasioned against Christian Charity on this the Holiest of Christian Feasts?

Yours faithfully,

G.J.C.

London SW19

25 April 1963

**To: Hugh Carleton Greene Esq. OBE, BBC,
London W1**

Dear Mr. Carleton Greene,

I do not think that a programme can be justified on the plea that it 'was intended as a light-hearted one' and that 'there was no intention of attacking religious belief or belittling the religious significance of Easter.'

Just consider for a moment what the position would have been if a similar skit had been presented on, for instance, the Jewish Day of Atonement, to take a religious festival that is, I suppose, neither more nor less sacred to Jews than Easter is sacred to Christians. The programme would have been accused of being anti-semitic and would have been very properly objected to. But is there any reason why the feelings of Christian people in the Country (who are, after all, in a majority compared with any other religious body) should not receive at least equal consideration to that which would be extended in similar circumstances to other religious groups?

Yours sincerely,

C.B.

Bluntisham, Huntingdon
29 September 1963

Dear Sir,

I wish to say how much I and all my family appreciate the return of That Was the Week etc. It is a great comfort and reassurance to know that the BBC can still have the courage to screen programmes of honesty and intelligence in the present climate of moronic hypocrisy.

I am not a person who frequently writes to the newspapers or the BBC, but I feel that it is very important that the BBC should know when there are many, many viewers who approve strongly of this series, who are not so quick to put pen to paper as members of some well-known 'pressure group' organisations. I hope that TW3 has a long and successful life ahead.

Yours faithfully,

P.J.B.

Lyndewode Road, Cambridge
30 September 1963

Dear Sir,

My people feel, as I do, that there is a place for satire in literature and broadcasting, and we have been interested in, and challenged by, the genuine satire in the programme. We have enjoyed the 'digs' at those in high places, and the mocking of pomposity. 'TW3' was a great idea and a worthwhile experiment. But it seemed that the first series gradually deteriorated, in that genuine satire was replaced by dirty-mindedness.

We had all hoped that something would be done to alter this before the new series started. You can judge, therefore, how disappointed we were with last Saturday evening's programme. The one genuine bit of satire was to the point – hurting, maybe – and certainly thought-provoking. For the rest, it was distressing to see the old familiar symptoms of adolescent dirty-mindedness reappearing, and – further – appalling bad taste in the photographic references to Dr. Stephen Ward and Mr. Profumo.

'TW3' is a programme which could be clever, as well as entertaining, and challenging too, with its frank comment on all facets of contemporary life. But this constant obsession with the dirty way of thinking of sex would seem to be yet another contribution to the lowering of moral standards.

Surely you can do better than this.

Yours sincerely,

(Rev.) A.B.

Colwyn Bay

3 October 1963

To: The Chairman, British Broadcasting Corporation, London W1

Dear Sir,

We watched with interest the return of TWTWTW to the air last Saturday night, in the hope that we might find it entertaining and perhaps instructive. In a Boarding School of some 400 teenage girls it is essential for the Staff to be 'with it'. We were bitterly disappointed. The show was occasionally funny, sometimes clever, but generally in bad taste and iconoclastic to the verge of idiocy. It is very easy to smash up The Establishment by picking mortar out from between the bricks. It is not so easy to build up another form of government to put in its place.

Perhaps we are flattering the young producer by overestimating the effect it has on the minds of twelve million viewers. Many of these are under 20 and so prone to accept without reflection any aspersions cast on authority. (We should know.) Hypocrisy and cant are every intelligent person's target, but they do not seem to us as dangerous as vandalism and nihilism.

A programme which started most successfully as 'Beyond the Fringe' has been inflated out of all proportion to its merits and now influences the political opinions and moral standards of perhaps a quarter of the youthful population of the country. It is high time it was taken off the air.

Yours faithfully,

C.S. Head Mistress
M. R. (Head of the French Department)

London SW1
14 October 1963

To: Donald Baverstock BBC Television Centre

Dear Mr Baverstock,

I have looked at one or two of the last 'TWTWTW' programmes and am perplexed by them. I have done my best, in the light of the controversy, to view them as impartially as possible, and I frankly dislike such points as, for example, the deliberate blasphemy of that item last Saturday about the Motor Show.

I viewed the programme the last two Saturdays with a quite representative party of six or eight people, mostly young – an art student, an English girl from South Africa, a young married woman who is a secretary, the manager of a West End theatre, a nurse, an author of children's books and one or two others. All of them were unanimous in commenting on the amateurishness of the programme. Its extraordinarily poor quality gave the impression of haste in preparation, and inexperience in production. Then we read in the papers – whether accurately or not – that the Negro comedian gets £100 a week. Is it conceivable, if this figure is right, that what he gave on Saturday is worth £100?

Surely if this type of programme is to be put over, men and women with some mature experience of entertaining the public could be enlisted rather than these seemingly untrained amateurs who give the impression that they are trying to make up for their inexperience by their shock tactics.

Yours faithfully,
R.W.W.

Britain's Bible Magazine, Brighton
17 October 1963

To: the Director General BBC
Dear Sir,

I am sorry to have to write this letter, for many are the hours of pleasure I have received from the programmes of the BBC but it is impossible to let an item in last night's 'TW3' go without making the strongest possible protest. It was the song Millicent Martin sang about contraception.

Recently an American comedian [Lenny Bruce] was refused permission to perform in this country on the grounds that he was a purveyor of 'sick' humour. I don't know what 'sick' humour is, but I do know that last night's song was sickening and that if that sort of thing continues we shall soon have a very sick society.

One has always looked to the B.B.C. for the maintenance of a good standard, but lately the use of objectionable language and questionable jokes has become increasingly frequent. If drunkenness, adultery and violence are practically the only occupations of the adult population, as our playwrights are at pains to inform us, then surely that is the very reason why you should try to raise the standard.

Yours truly,
J.W.

Great Sutton, Wirral

13 October 1963

To: The Director, B.B.C. Television, Shepherd's Bush W12

Dear Sir,

Last month you were quoted on the B.B.C. sound news service as saying that the show 'That was the week that was' would continue through the Autumn, but 'with the smut taken out'. The smut should never have been there in the first place.

How far your directions are being obeyed and observed will become apparent to you when you read the script of last night's broadcast of the programme. It has altered not a jot since you gave your promise to the viewers a month ago. Take away the swearing, the sneering, the smearing and the lechery and all you will have is a drab negative little programme which is neither instructive nor entertaining.

There was a time when I felt a great pride in the B.B.C., and gratitude for its sense of responsibility and integrity. Under your direction the Television Service is showing little of either quality. May we please see some determined and constructive action on your part to set your house in order.

Yours faithfully,

E.B.W.L.

Amersham, Buckinghamshire

20 October 1963

To: Carlton Greene Esq., O.B.E., Director General, British Broadcasting Corporation, Langham Place, London W1

Dear Sir,

Both my wife and I are thoroughly disgusted with the appallingly vulgar, impertinent and vicious attack made on Lord Home last evening during the programme 'This is the Week that Was'. [sic]

Indeed, the whole thing is quite beyond the standards one expects in a British Programme – the whole thing was quite stupid but the liberties taken last night are far too excessive.

How these people are allowed to get away with such vile and filthy attacks on personalities is quite beyond our comprehension and one can only hope that this time some definite action will be taken against the offenders.

I have sent copies of this letter to Mr. Ronald Bell, the member for South Bucks and also the Post Master General.

Yours faithfully,

D. K.

Sevenoaks, Kent

27 October 1963

To: Charles Curran, General Advisory Council, B.B.C. W1

Dear Mr. Curran,

After seeing last Saturday's programme 'That was the Week that was' and reading your statement in today's 'Sunday Telegraph', I simply cannot understand how you can say that this programme is now clean.

I enjoy humour and I am all for genuine satire, but I could only smile once during this programme. Several numbers, such as the 'Virgins Anonymous' song and the one by an apparently nude man and a girl in a bath, were simple incitement to promiscuity. A friend from France was with me and I must say I was deeply ashamed that this was the level of humour our national broadcasting corporation now offers. You must surely agree that this sort of thing is simply decadent and must strike other countries as in line with the worst they have thought about us after the Profumo Scandal.

As for the attack on the Church as 'Big Business', that was in the worst taste. It showed up the extreme Left Wing, atheist bias of the producers of this programme. Many reforms are needed in the Church, as I would be the first to admit, but I feel sure thousands of last night's viewers must have been left with the same impression as I was: this was not a humorous tilting at what was wrong, but a planned attempt to split the people from the Church. The Church remains at least one repository of sound faith and moral backbone in the country. Without these, our culture will soon die, like a tree cut off at the roots. And even good humour goes out of the window, as it did last night.

Yours sincerely,

G. D.

London SE23

14 November 1963

To: The Board of Governors, B.B.C., Broadcasting House, W1

Dear Sirs,

As an ardent and devoted fan of B.B.C. Television, I write to protest most strongly at the decision to take off T.W.3 at the end of December, and particularly at the reason given. I am reasonably sure that absolutely no-one will believe that the fact that 1964 is [an] election year is the only reason why we are to be denied this form of comment. After all, this fact was known when the programme came back in September and if the election is delayed until late in the year we are being defrauded rather early.

I can't honestly say I always enjoyed the programme, but with many others I felt that it helped to guard us in some way against pomposity and cynical exploitation from the top brass.

I sincerely hope that the Governors will relent, or at least will reassure us that this type of programme will return without any clipping of claws.

Yours sincerely,

(Miss) A. M. D.

Ashford, Kent

17 November 1963

Dear Sir,

It appears that the B.B.C. is swayed by individual pleas and the fact that there were 810 complaints after the 'Disraeli speech' in TW3 has been largely responsible for the sudden decision to discontinue the show. I wonder if you take into account the fact that it is human nature to complain more than to commend?

Anyway, I now see it as a duty as one of the MILLIONS who have not complained, to write and say how very disappointed we are that Saturday, the dreariest day of the B.B.C. week, is to lose its one bright spot and to beg you to reconsider. Why not start TW3 at mid-night?

If we had written before, it would have been with mixed feelings of delight and disgruntlement but above all of gratitude to the B.B.C. for providing something so vitally alive and kicking. Often it was too long, sometimes 'ill-humoured', only four of those taking part were worthy of their responsibilities, many of the 'sketches' were so feeble that they would have foundered even if performed by artists of a different calibre. (One would have liked to see Dora Brian [sic] Ron Moody, Alfred Marks, Michael Bentine, Bea Lillie etc. in TW3!)

Fumbled by the less effective members of the team, they [the sketches] could and did die several times over but there was always something in the programme that made it more worthwhile watching

There was, at first at any rate, an uninhibited lifting of the heavy lid of respectability from the Establishment dustbin. That this was being allowed by, of all bodies, the B.B.C. made one feel proud, for once, to be British. Surely making the show [start] earlier was a mistake and automatically produced more adverse criticism by bringing it under the noses of those who were 'not ready for it'?

Yours faithfully,

J. E.

Oxted, Surrey

17 November 1963

Dear Sir,

TWTWTW last Saturday with its song on contraceptives, and the choir boy singing 'now thank we all our God' in connection with Courtaulds, was just about as dirty as dirt can go. Yours is a wise decision to have it off, but I thought this series to have been cleaned up. Whoever vets the programme must have been asleep on Saturday. I was surprised that the reason given for TWTWTW being discontinued was political, not moral. The criticisms were always of the lack of moral standards.

It's good to see you continue with the favourites in entertainment:- Harry Worth, Perry Mason, The Lucy Show, and The Defenders. They have a standard.

Yours,

R. C.

St. Stephens House, Westminster SW1

25 November 1963

To: Director General British Broadcasting Corporation W1

Dear Mr Hugh Carleton Greene,

I am writing to you because I was so much impressed with the TW3 Programme last Saturday that I feel I must express my thanks and admiration to all concerned. I do not generally care for this programme although I sometimes find some of it amusing, but this was really outstanding.

It seems to me that no better means of expressing the feelings of the British people on the assassination of President Kennedy could be found than to offer this recording to the U.S. networks.

Yours sincerely,

Major General Sir Edward Spears K.B.E. M.C.

Telegram from:

East Bergholt Essex 8 December 1963

To: The Director General BBC London

SUPERB PERFORMANCE BY TWTWTW TONIGHT STOP SURELY YOU CANT SUPPRESS THIS BECAUSE OF THE WINDYNESS OF POLITICIANS IN AN ELECTION YEAR

QUERY YOUR ADVISERY [sic] COUNCIL IS BIGGEST BODY
OF SPOIL SPORTS IN COUNTRY STOP POLITICIANS
PARTICULARLY IN ELECTION YEAR NEED GUIDANCE
AS TO HOW TO ENTERTAIN PUBLIC STOP IF YOU
PERSEVERE IN YOUR ABSURD DECISION YOU WILL BE
DOING A NATIONAL DISSERVICE TO THE PUBLIC AND TO
THE POLITICIANS = RANDOLPH CHURCHIL =

> Brocket Hall, Welwyn, Herts.
> 29 December 1963

To: Sir Arthur fforde, Chairman,
B.B.C. Langham Place W1

Dear Sir Arthur,

I am sorry to have to write to you again about T.W.3 but at any
rate it will be the last time during this series. I trust it may be the
last time ever.

Last night's performance, which I hope you saw, excelled
[exceeded?] even the previous performances in vulgarity and
blasphemy.

Lady Brocket and I who are personal friends of Princess
Alexandra and Mr. Angus Ogilvie, do not regard it as amusing
when among other wedding presents it was stated that 'Angus
Ogilvie gave her a baby'. We are also not amused at a scene in
which Millicent Martin appeared concerned with 'fly buttons
being undone.'

Other remarks, including those about the Queen, made us feel
very relieved that last night was the last performance of this series,
and we devoutly hope that such a series will not again appear.

I am sorry to say so, but very many people feel that murders,
thefts and many other crimes are encouraged by Television, and
I only wish that programmes could be checked on a much more
severe basis before being shown to the public.

With best wishes for the New Year,

Yours sincerely,

(Sgd) [Lord] BROCKET

CHAPTER TEN

THE PROFUMO AFFAIR

In June 1963, between the two series of *TW3*, John Profumo resigned as Minister of State for War. In March, he had made a personal statement to the House of Commons in which he had denied any impropriety in his relationship with model and showgirl Christine Keeler. Three months later, in the wake of constant rumours that simply would not stop even when he threatened libel actions against any organisation that published them, he was forced to admit that he had lied to the Commons.

The Conservative Party was in meltdown. 'A great party is not to be brought down by a proven liar and a woman of easy virtue,' shouted Lord Hailsham. A scapegoat was necessary to draw the heat away from Macmillan, the government and the Conservatives with a general election only a year away. Stephen Ward – osteopath, sketch artist and full-time hedonist – had introduced Keeler to Profumo in August 1961 when they met at the swimming pool outside Lord Astor's stately home, Cliveden. Ward, along with the two young women to whom he had offered accommodation, Keeler and Mandy Rice-Davies, were at the centre of the subsequent scandalous revelations and hence the obvious candidates. The girls were threatened with prison; Ward was arrested.

Ward was charged with living off their immoral earnings although it was perfectly clear to everyone that although they slept with men quite promiscuously and accepted money or dinners from them, they were not professional prostitutes and Ward was not their pimp. The Establishment, however, in a year that saw the Great Train Robbery in which the public took the side of the robbers as well as its merciless lampooning by *TW3*, was determined to have its revenge. The biased summing-up of the judge left Ward in no doubt that he would be found guilty and imprisoned. The humiliation and unfairness was impossible to bear. The night before the jury was due to return he took an overdose of sleeping pills.

The case had caused the BBC some problems as the following letters make clear. The Profumo Affair, as it had come to be called, was yet another indication that society was moving in a new and strange direction. Upper class men had long enjoyed their dalliances with lower class girls but rarely had the news been spread over the popular press. News of orgies attended by High Court judges and prostitutes and of whipping parties in Mayfair were printed alongside *The Times* Law Reports and the county cricket scoreboard. Newspapers realised that there was an insatiable thirst for knowledge of the details of the affair, and for the revelations of the girls' behaviour in Ward's flat in Wimpole Mews. Christine Keeler sold her story to the *News of the World* for £23,000, an unheard-of sum for the time.

The BBC was faced with the problem of reporting the details of the trial on its news bulletins. The detail was undoubtedly salacious but the detail was what most people wanted to learn. The BBC could choose to edit its reports to omit some of the salacious detail, but it prided itself on presenting the news impartially and in full. Its distinguished reputation really rested on the manner in which it had dealt with the news during the dark days of World War II.

There is no doubt that had John Reith still been its Director General, not a hint of the two-way mirrors permitting viewers a sight of the sexual shenanigans allegedly going on at Wimpole Mews would have been broadcast. Reith, however, was long gone and in his place sat Hugh Carleton Greene, a man with a very different approach to public morality. As Stephen Ward stood in the dock and BBC reporters told their listeners and viewers what had been said in court, the letters began …

London EC4

28 June 1963

To: The Director General, B.B.C., Portland Place, London W1

Dear Sir,

This is to confirm my telephone call at 6.30pm this evening to your Duty Officer, in the News Room, expressing my husband's and my disgust at the first item in the six o'clock News this evening. For about six minutes we had the details of what Miss Keeler wore in Court, the men she had slept with and so on. There can be no justification for compelling us to listen to all this before coming to the serious news, there was no question of National security or other public interest to be served.

We hope that you will yourself personally ensure that the normal high standards maintained by and expected of the B.B.C. will in future be adhered to.

Happily we were alone in our home at the time. Had we had young people with us as is sometimes the case, we would have been very embarrassed, and there must be millions of homes where the six o'clock news is a family event and where this nauseating stuff had to be listened to.

Faithfully,

Mrs. M. J.

Calne, Wiltshire

28 June 1963

To: The Editor, News, B.B.C., Broadcasting House, London

Dear Sir,

Both as a parent of young children and as a Headmaster I wish to register a very strong protest at the reporting of the [Stephen] Ward case given on the 6 o'clock news of the B.B.C. sound programme today.

The selection of items, their presentation and the amount of absolutely gratuitous detail seemed, to my incredulous ears, to have reduced the whole thing to a standard of sensationalism worthy of the most sordid elements of the gutter press. The whole tone of the report, not excluding the announcer's expressive voice, could not fail, in my opinion, to have a most corrupting influence on the minds of young people who might well be expected to join their parents in listening to the six o'clock news.

Apart from the frequent references to intercourse, the following points are among those I found most offensive:

1. The reference to the fitting of the mirror and its purpose, with the detail 'he hoped people would pay to come and watch.'

2. The quotation of Ward's comments to Miss Keeler about other girls (what sort of news is this?)

3. The glorification of the two witnesses (themselves involved in these disgusting forms of vice) implicit in the description of their costumes, including gloves! This sort of thing might be news for the lower gutter press but surely not for the B.B.C.

Is it too much to ask that the B.B.C. should consider that they have serious responsibilities to the family circle in their 6 o'clock news bulletins (T.V. or sound)?

Yours faithfully,

N. T.

National Council of Women of Great Britain
23 July 1963

To: Hugh Carleton Greene Esq., Broadcasting House, London W1

Dear Mr. Greene,

My Council wishes to register a strong protest against the way in which the news of the Profumo affair, and of the preliminary hearing of the case against Dr. Stephen Ward was presented both on radio and television.

While the National Council of Women appreciates that news should not be withheld from the public, it is strongly felt that far more detail was given than was necessary.

My Council is of the opinion that Radio and Television are not suitable media for the detailed presentation of such subject matter.

Yours sincerely,

C. G.

The New Daily London WC1
22 July 1963

To: Director-General, British Broadcasting Corporation, London W1

Dear Mr. Carleton Green,

The sordid and unsavoury Ward case is expected to open at the Old Bailey to-day. We believe we speak for millions of people when we ask you to give instructions that it shall not be reported on radio and television in a way that will cause embarrassment and offence in the homes into which your broadcasts go.

What we are asking is that, particularly on the six o'clock news when millions of children are still up, words and phrases shall not be used that cause embarrassment. The phrase to which objection was taken during the Police Court case was chiefly 'intercourse' and 'sexual intercourse'. Mothers said that they had been asked by children of seven and eight who heard it on the news to explain what it meant. [Also] that your reports shall not glamourise common prostitutes by describing their appearance and what they are wearing.

Everybody who installs a radio or television set pays a licence fee does so on the implied understanding that certain standards shall be maintained. You are the guardian of those standards.

If you wish to refresh your memory as to what they are please read the Dedication in the Entrance Hall to Broadcasting House placed there by Sir John Reith in 1931, and particularly the phrase 'that all things hostile to peace and purity may be banished from this House.'

Sincerely yours,

E. M.

CHAPTER ELEVEN

NOT SO MUCH A PROGRAMME, MORE A WAY OF LIFE

That Was the Week That Was ended its second and final series just after Christmas 1963. The BBC placed it into permanent limbo on the grounds that 1964 was an election year and political satire might affect the Corporation's impartiality, a claim that was fiercely disputed by the show's supporters. However, there remained a desire to retain as much as possible of what had made the original programme a success, so Frost returned the following autumn with Willie Rushton and a number of new performers – John Bird (who would have presented *TW3* in preference to the unknown Frost had he not been previously booked to go to the United States), John Fortune, John Wells and Eleanor Bron.

The programme was made up of a mixture of sketches and conversation and it was transmitted three times a week, late at night on Friday, Saturday and Sunday. As with *TW3*, the opening song (sung by three different singers on the three nights that constituted the weekend) contained the convoluted title and the menu of what was to follow:

> Not so much a programme
> More a way of life
> And a way of looking
> At the world
> One eye opened wide
> One eye closed
> And between the two the picture gets composed.

There was much that was well received in the new format. John Bird's impersonation of Harold Wilson, the new prime minister, was better than Mike Yarwood's because it had more political bite, but his politically incorrect caricature of an East African politician, though greatly enjoyed at the time, would never have been allowed on the screen a decade or two later. Eleanor Bron played Lady Pamela Stitty, a well-meaning lady of the Conservative party, a running character invented by Peter Cook.

The chat show's regular guests resembled a Ned Sherrin dinner party: Harvey Orkin, an American talent agent; the eminent philosopher A.J. Ayer and his American wife, the newspaper columnist Dee Wells; Mark Boxer, the founding editor of the influential *Sunday Times* colour magazine; and, perhaps most successfully, the witty, stuttering Irish aristocrat Patrick Campbell, later one of the captains on *Call My Bluff*. Bernard Levin returned to cause more widespread fury, particularly when he insulted Sir Alec Douglas-Home, the Leader of the Opposition, by calling him an imbecile and a cretin. It was undoubtedly cruel, but it sprang from the former prime minister's admission that his knowledge of economics was so poor that he tried to understand the nation's finances with the use of matchsticks. He was the last of the grouse moor Etonian Tory leaders. The following year the party elected the grammar-school educated Ted Heath as its new leader.

Not So Much a Programme began in November 1964, a month after Harold Wilson entered Downing Street for the first time, but it was not considered a success. Despite the BBC's initial encouragement, *NSMAPMAWOL* did not trip off the tongue as lightly as *TW3* and the series came to an end, largely unmourned, in April 1965. By this time David Frost was building his career in the United States, and when Sherrin returned with a new late-night Saturday show in the autumn of 1965, the presenter was not Frost but Robert Robinson.

However, *Not So Much a Programme* attracted more correspondence than its 21-week run appeared to have warranted. The outraged reaction to three sketches makes up the bulk of the complaints. The skewering of the Duke of Windsor, a sketch transmitted within hours of the death of his sister, the Princess Royal, has already been referred to in the section on the Royal Family. Levin's attack on Douglas-Home provoked considerable sympathy for the man who had been on the side of the Guilty Men of Munich in 1938, but the overwhelming response was to a sketch about birth control.

This was transmitted just over halfway through the run of the series, but by that time the programme had succeeded in getting up the noses of a number of correspondents as it widened its range of targets to include professions who had previously thought themselves safe when attacks were concentrated on the church, the monarchy and parliament. No longer. Even town planners were now considered ripe for satire.

Newport, Monmouthshire
8 December 1964

To: David Frost Esq., c/o Broadcasting House London W1

Dear Sir,

I refer to the Sunday evening edition of 'Not So Much a Programme, More a Way of Life' and to your discussion about town planning. I am particularly concerned about the remarks made by Norman St. John Stevas to the effect that there is no profession of town planning and that no training is required to become a town planner.

This is completely wrong. There is a Chartered Town Planning Institute which requires its members to take Intermediate and Final Examinations of a standard comparable to those of R.I.C.S and R.I.BA. The preparation and tuition for these examinations normally takes five to six years.

Town planning tends to be devalued and not given the importance it deserves. This process has been aided by the Conservative Government's attitude during their years in office and is given additional boost every time people such as St. John Stevas give voice to ill-considered and inaccurate statements.

I must add in conclusion that although I am a Chartered Town Planner the views I have expressed in this letter are my own and do not represent those of the Town Planning Institute or the Local Authority by which I am employed.

Yours faithfully,

P.R.O.

London SW2

22 November 1964

To: The Controller The BBC, Broadcasting House, London W1

Dear Sir,

As one who has always been proud to be British, and as a Grandfather of 9 grandchildren I must protest most seriously at the production which the BBC allowed to be shown under the heading of 'Not so much a Programme more a way of life', at 10.25pm last Friday.

The production was allowed to be an insult to decent people, the coloured gentleman who insulted us 'Right, left and Centre' has done more harm to relations between White and Coloured persons than any chalking on the wall could have done and everybody whom I have met during the last 2 days whom [sic] saw that programme are oddly enough entirely of the same opinion as myself so I cannot be very wrong in my complaint and they too await a reply to this letter of absolute disgust.

I am just an ordinary small businessman, I have been a Long Distance Lorry driver, a London Bus Driver, a Flight Lieutenant in the R.A.F. and now run a small Private Hire Business and I have Great Regard for Great Britain and the Commonwealth and its people, white and coloured and I am aware of the difficulties of us living together in harmony.

David Frost and his 'warped' cast especially the coloured gentleman, insults the common decency of all clean minded people of all classes. May I respectfully ask you to give me your own opinion on the manner in which our Coloured gentleman insulted all intelligent minded people last Friday night and whether this sort of thing will be allowed again.

Yours truly,

J.E.P.

Exclusive Private Hire by Rolls Royce Limousines for all occasions

Chatsworth, Bakewell, Derbyshire
22 November 1964

Dear Greene,

As a former member of the B.B.C. Advisory Council I write to say how horrified I was by the item called a political broadcast by the fascist party included in the programme 'Not so much a programme, more a way of life'.

For sheer appalling bad taste I have never seen its equal. Perhaps that is what you wish the B.B.C. to achieve.

Yours?

Sincerely,

[the Duke of] Devonshire

From: The Most Reverend Archbishop Lord Fisher of Lambeth, Trent Rectory, Sherborne, Dorset

23 November 1964

To: Sir Hugh Greene, The B.B.C., Broadcasting House, Portland Place, London W1

My dear Greene,

You very kindly allow me to write a personal letter to you when the spirit moves me. May I say I was deeply moved or rather distressed by the defence which you gave in an answer to a complaint from the High Commissioner of Kenya; caused by a reference to [President of Kenya] Jomo Kenyatta in a B.B.C. programme which was 'Not so much a Programme as [sic] A Way of Life'.

It used to be thought that when a neighbour complains of something as a personal insult the proper way to reply was to say – I am sorry –. Knowing the whole history of our relations with Africans in general and Kenya in particular it seems to me just simply deplorable that you should defend David Frost & Co. instead of saying wholeheartedly that you are sorry.

I do not watch this programme but I did on the night after the offence by accident see the beginning of it in which David Frost added a little impertinent insult to the injury already done. And all this adds to the intensely difficult task of establishing relations of trust and friendship between emergent Africans and our complex country.

Perhaps I should add that in a world so interrelated as this it is really terribly insensitive to suppose that Kenyatta should have the same sense of humour about a political caricature as we have!

Yours sincerely,
Fisher of Lambeth

London NW10
4 January 1965

Dear Mr. Frost,

I write this letter as a devotee of 'Not So Much a Programme' and as a humble PC of the Metropolitan Police. Being a policeman necessarily means missing a fair number of your programmes but this is just one of the many crosses we have to bear in common with Miss [novelist and critic Brigid] Brophy's careless remarks on Sunday.

Miss Brophy represents a fair cross-section of the populace with whom the police unfortunately have to deal all year round – stupidity, ignorance, resentment, malice and downright hatred are part and parcel of every policeman's working day.

Being on one's feet for 12 or 14 hours (on C.N.D. demonstrations) and then being pushed around by long haired loud-mouths is hardly likely to improve one's demeanour. Although the general prescription these days is that the policeman is a mindless moron with a truncheon for smashing heads in, boots for fracturing ribs and a tongue for the purposes of committing perjury, I am an apparent exception.

I loathe the use of violence and could not in all conscience remain in an organisation that encouraged or permitted the use of it. Your film, showing Negroes kicked whilst bound and helpless, sickened me. We (myself and other officers) do however enjoy Mr. Rushton's antics. Good luck to him. No one could take him seriously.

Miss Brophy's little saga on the [arrested] 70 year old woman broke my callous heart. Salty tears dripped into the pint of Beatnik's blood I customarily drink before retiring for the night. In this big, big heart of mine I always find room to forgive eccentrics like Miss Brophy.

Yours sincerely,

J. M.

Edinburgh

19 January 1965

To: Ned Sherrin Esq. Producer and Director, BBC, London

Dear Sir,

The lack of a 'normal' woman in your programme seems inexcusable in this day of well-educated and well spoken women.

The rather curious specimens whom you have so far presented on rare occasions make this female viewer uncomfortable, for they either dress, think and speak oddly or/and have a negligible contribution to make to the discussion.

Admittedly, the male members of the speaking panel are often trite, though that may be the fault of the questions and Mr Frost but I simply refuse to believe that there are no intelligent, gracious women able and willing to enhance the existing male, cigarette/cigar smoking, all but shirt-sleeved panel of 'visitors'.

Yours faithfully,

M. E. M. (Miss)

Skegness Lincolnshire
2 February 1965

Dear Sirs,

Not so much a programme, more a way of life

With reference to the remark made in your programme of January 31st.

If Mr. Mossman implied that Skegness is not bracing, evidentially he does not know what he is talking about. Perhaps he has never sampled the air of Skegness, and we take this opportunity of inviting him to our resort.

Our slogan is not misleading, and means exactly what it says. It has been scientifically proved that the nature of the air on this stretch of coast is bracing.

Yours faithfully,

H.L.C.
Skegness Hoteliers Association.

London SW8
26 February 1965

To: Programme Department
BBC Television Centre Wood Lane W.12

Dear Sirs,

Just for the record – here is one viewer who considers 'Not So Much ... ' is the only 'adult entertainment' programme the BBC offers at the present time. Half its attraction is the fact that it runs three nights each week, and if the BBC kills this programme I, for one, will be very cross.

Yours faithfully,

J. B.

Liverpool 18
28 February 1965

Dear Sir,

I watched your programme last Saturday night and was completely sickened by the sketch you showed of the Irish woman and the priest.

I did not find the general vulgarity of the setting amusing. Why did you show the priest taking the money? I thought you were trying to hit at the Church's attitude to Birth Control. Obviously you couldn't resist other malicious jabs in the process.

The discussion about another baby was absolutely revolting; both this and the discussion of the methods of Birth Control could never take place. Perhaps worst of all were the inferences made e.g. the priest's support of the drunken husband.

I grew to dislike the woman – Dee something – [newspaper columnist and broadcaster Dee Wells] who wouldn't allow Norman St. John Stevas to defend his church's attitude which had just been attacked. I wonder why the audience clapped when she called him 'a silly man'. She reminded me of the female astrologer who once squirted a lemon at Bernard Levin on TW.

I don't think I shall watch your programme again.

Yours sincerely,

Anon

Liverpool 19
1 March 1965

To: BBC, Broadcasting House London

Dear Sir,

As an erstwhile Catholic who saw the sketch on Saturday night and also enjoyed Miss Dee Wells' valuable contribution to the later discussion, I am amazed at the reaction of Mr. Simon Mahon and his fellow M.P.s.

Just after the First World War, I collected rents in the Dockland area of Liverpool, and saw the misery and suffering caused by un-employment to the men and women with large families. It was common practice for one 'affluent' family, invariably with several bullies of sons, to pay the rent of say five or six houses and charge interest of twopence in the shilling. To obtain the loan a 'compulsory' purchase of one shilling's worth of 'not so fresh fish' was made. This 'Protection' racket was a Godsend to the victims, in as much as it kept a roof over their heads. The moneylenders were nearly always 'Pillars of the Church'. I never heard of the Church taking part in a Public Outcry against the deplorable conditions lived in by the people. One day a woman told me she had no rent, no bread in the house and only one penny. The priest called whilst I was there and she handed him the penny – and he took it!

In my Mother's day the wages of Dockland were paid out in the Public houses and it was usual to see children waiting outside for the miserable pittances to take home to their mothers before the brewers got the lot. Small blame on the men but large blame on the Church who fought hard against the working class and Socialism (the Anti-Christ). The Labour Party grew in Liverpool from the struggle of Dockland [and] made the safe seats for those M.P.s who are now ashamed of its source.

Yours faithfully,

M. F. M. (Mrs.)

Liverpool 14

2 March 1965

To: Mr. Huw Wheldon, Controller of Television Programmes BBC Shepherd's Bush London W12

Dear Sir,

I have long grown accustomed to the barrage of wholesale dishonesty, cowardly insinuation, and unadulterated filth which emanated from producers and 'artists' of B.B.C. television programmes. However, the cesspool of mental and moral degradation from which ideas for many of your programmes are drawn can rarely have vomited such a nauseating, disgusting, offensive and insulting piece of shameful and insolent effrontery as the 'Birth Control' sketch last Saturday night. Clearly, the much vaunted B.B.C. is riddled with the cancer of iniquity, and needs to be purged of some very corrupt and feeble-minded fools.

I am a Catholic who worked for the first seven years (1956–63) in St Joseph's Parish Liverpool. Some of the scoundrels harboured by your institution would have benefitted from being brought up in a Liverpool 'slum'. Their arrogance, pomposity and fabricated claptrap would have been strangled long before they had a chance to become the arch-contaminators of the nation, paraded on our screens by a conceited and quite un-British Broadcasting Corporation.

With utter contempt for the instigators of this shabby, pitiful and despicable episode,

I am, Sir,

Yours faithfully,

Rev. L. J. M.

Hay-On-Wye, Hereford

2 March 1965

To: The Director General BBC Television Programmes
Not So Much A Programme, More a Way of Life

Dear Sir,

I have read a report on the front page of the 'Daily Mail' of to-day's date to the effect that you are likely, at the instigation of three Members of Parliament (two Labourites and one Tory), to be asked to apologise publicly for some highly topical, and highly truthful, allusions to certain practices of the Church of Rome which received attention (and not before time) in last Saturday's programme.

May I congratulate you on this much needed publicity? May I also express the hope that you will apologise for nothing, and that you will adhere to the good old War-Cry of 'No Surrender'? It would be a very sad day that you were compelled to restrict your programmes to what is acceptable to the Pope's Brass Band.

Yours very truly

W.M.E.A.

copy to Mr. Simon Mahon MP House of Commons

Liverpool & District Catholic Young Men's Society
Amateur Football League Under the Patronage of
His Grace the Archbishop of Liverpool
3 March 1965

Dear Sir,

At the Monthly General Meeting of the above League, held at St.
Francis Xavier's Men's Club on Monday last, under the item Other
Business, the following resolution was passed, with acclamation.

'We, the members of the Liverpool & District C.Y.M.S. Amateur
Football League, wish to protest in the strongest possible terms
concerning the slanderous and disgusting sketch which defiled the
BBC Programme & Television Service, in the series, 'Not so much
a Programme, More a way of Life'. It casts an unwarranted slur on
the Catholic people of Liverpool and Merseyside and on the English
and Irish Clergy who dedicate themselves to the service of the
Community in the area. We feel that a very full apology should be
made and an assurance that such programmes will not be repeated.'

B.E.J.

Coventry
4 March 1965

Dear Sirs,

We were thoroughly disgusted to read that Sir Hugh Greene
apologised to the M.P.'s concerned due to the Catholic sketch in
'N.S.M.a P'.

The M.P.'s have no right what-so-ever to ask for an apology
as they either objected to the sketch on the grounds of being a
Catholic or are afraid of losing votes as Liverpool has so many
Catholics in its community. On both counts this is no reason for
demanding apologies.

This month we shall have our second child and do not wish
to have anymore due to the world population crisis. Why should
our children's children be starving just to support people who are
frightened of a stupid religious belief?

Yours faithfully,

J. E. H. (Mrs.)

Rhos-on-Sea, Colwyn Bay
5 March 1965

Dear Mr. Frost,

I am glad that you are not backing down to Lord Longford and the rest of the idiots who are asking for a public apology – the R.C. sketch last weekend, because it was absolutely 'spot on'.

I have actually been present when this has happened and the RC priest accepted quite a large sum (it looked like £20) from a chap who was able to eke out a precarious living in a café in Colwyn Bay.

I also saw the mother of a large family, whose husband was a labourer at the Lancashire Steel Corporation give the RC priest a £1 note and he accepted it with ill grace. It made me realise what a phoney religion this is. 'I reckon all RCs are either 'nutcases' or making money out of it.

[Please] turn off the sound from your vocals, your songs are bloody awful. Why not have a good tenor (British) singing 'My Dreams'? I am sure your audience would be thrilled to bits.

Best of good wishes,

Yours sincerely,

E. J.

Brechin, Angus
5 March 1965

To: David Frost Esq., B.B.C., London W1
Dear Mr.Frost

R.C. Birth Control Sketch

Let me start by saying how much I enjoy your programme & that I was among those many who felt almost that they had lost a blowsy old friend when dear & vulgar, but nonetheless thought-provoking and funny TW3 went off the air. However Not So Much a Programme promises to be even better: this mainly because the other side is given a fair crack of the whip.

This is among the few programmes which we ever find it worthwhile to watch.

Having said all this, it is remarkable having the discernment which is yours, how the show can go off the rails; this particularly in the case of the above sketch. I can assure you that those who protest are by no means 'a minority of a minority'. On birth control I could not disagree more fundamentally than I do with the present attitude of the R.C. Church.

Ridiculing the opposition so savagely has the reverse effect of what is intended. It was far off the mark in its picture of the RC priest taking so much money from a poor family. One dispenses everything from bunches of spring flowers to the odd bottle of sherry to brighten the lives of those who live alone in single rooms. We refuse daily to take subscriptions or to ask for expenses incurred from those who cannot afford them. I am sorry to sound like a schoolmaster but anything so bold is bound to drop the odd clanger from time to time. Only having done so, it might be as well to admit it.

With best wishes,

(Rev.) L.J.A.B.
P.S. We miss Eleanor Bron

Great Ormsby, Norfolk
6 March 1965

Sir,

Could I say how much I laughed at the sketch about the Catholic priest and the mother with a regiment of children, Sat 27th February. I can't understand what all the fuss is about from such men as Lord Longford. Maybe if he had his way we would be back to the gloomy Sundays of my boyhood days. I am now 65. I liked your spirited reply, Daily Mail, March 5th and please, let's have a bit more of this sort of thing.

Sincerely,

D.B.M.C. (Mrs.)

11 March 1965

To: The Director of the BBC

I should think you might apologise for the silliest, most repulsive, filthiest and depraved skit I have ever seen during my life on this earth. Have sensible discussions about birth control by all means (and other controversial topics) but only discussions. To preface a talk on such a subject with a filthy skit indicates something wrong at the top with the BBC. We have to pay our licences, so I should think we might have some say in the programmes – or do we have to pander to some pathetic desire to be bold, modern, and 'with it'?

'Not so much' is only looked at by me as I love the brilliance of John Bird – the rest of it is largely tripe – and that nightmare song!

yours,

R. B.

Stockport, Cheshire

12 March 1965

Dear Mr. Frost,

This is not a fan letter but a serious query arising out of a discussion which I had with a friend recently. We are sixth-formers and have watched both 'That Was the Week That Was' and 'Not so much a programme, more a way of life' regularly. TW3 was at times destructive but we feel 'Not so much a programme' achieved a higher standard and does have something more constructive to offer.

In discussing this we began to examine what we considered the motive for satire ought to be and more particularly, what your own personal motives were. We decided that you were either a rebel, an idealist or have a gigantic chip on your shoulder and enjoy making trouble. Otherwise you simply have a vicious nature or are in it for the money.

Yours sincerely,

M. L.

Prittlewell, Essex
26 March 1965 11.30 p.m.

To: Mr. David Frost, B.B.C.

It is impossible for me to go to bed without protesting about the unwarranted attack by Bernard Levin on Sir Alex [sic] Douglas Home, who is a man of integrity and culture and would never be guilty of such a breach of good taste.

Ten minutes before he was indulging in a diatribe against [the] privilege of free speech in the House of Commons. I assume that he considers Bernard Levin – being a superior being, not subject to ordinary laws – may be allowed the privilege of publicly insulting anybody. Big congratulations and thanks to Paddy who restored ordinary logic and civility to the programme.

P.B.H.

London W6
28 March 1965

For the attention of Sir Hugh Carleton-Greene

Dear Sir,

I write to confirm a telephone call I had with your Duty Officer at 2345 hours on Friday night. Some years ago I had occasion to write to you when systematically and deliberately, TW3 set out to destroy the public image of Mr Macmillan, a show with which Ned Sherrin and David Frost were associated. In this they succeeded and at the time I believe I used the words 'character assassination.' As soon as Mr Macmillan disappeared the target of the attack switched to Sir Alec Douglas Home.

On Friday we were treated to an attack on privilege in parliament by Bernard Levin who gratuitously introduced into the conversation the fact that Sir Alec Douglas Home was 'a cretin'. When challenged by [Irish journalist, humourist and later panel captain on *Call My Bluff*] Patrick Campbell, there was no withdrawal by Levin.

The BBC provides a platform night after night for public attacks on the character, mental strength and integrity of Sir Alec Douglas Home. By refusing to act when I last wrote to you, you allowed TW3 to destroy Macmillan. My letter received a formal acknowledgement but although my letter was addressed to you, you did not have either the grace or the courtesy to reply to me in person. This time I would welcome a personal response.

Yours faithfully,

I.H.B.

London S.W.1

29 March 1965

To: Not So Much a Programme More a Way of Life, BBC, Broadcasting House, Portland Place London W.1

Dear Sirs,

Until Friday night I was a fan of your show 'Not So Much a Programme etc.' but it is completely beyond me how you can invite such a revolting pig (and quite frankly there is no other word for the man) as Bernard Levin on your show. To let such a creature speak about the former Prime Minister of England in the manner he did and do NOTHING about it – completely amazes me. I also found your skit on Vietnam discusting [sic] and then, last night, a couple of hours after the death of the Princess Royal, you dared to show that tasteless skit about the Duke and Duchess of Windsor. Have you no respect for anybody or anything?

I sincerely hope this programme will be taken off the air as soon as possible, and with it David Frost forever. I for one assure you I will never watch it again.

Yours sincerely,

S. T.

Clevedon, Somerset

30 March 1965

To: Mr. N. Sherrin BBC Television Centre Wood Lane London W.12

Dear Sir,

It is with great pleasure we read that 'Not so much a Programme' is to be killed off.

Those responsible for this programme should have been drowned in their own Cess-pits long ago.

If Frost and his crowd had seen, and gone through one hundredth part of what the Duke of Windsor and many thousands of his age group had had to stomach, they would have needed more than one change of under-pants.

It is to be hoped that the satire put over in America is on American life – Even the lowest animal rarely bites the hand that feeds it.

Yours faithfully,

C. H. H.
Copy sent to:-
The Daily Mail
The Daily Express
Points of View

London W3

30 March 1965

To: Sir Hugh Greene, BBC, Wood Lane, London W12

Dear Sir,

I was amazed to read in the newspapers that 'after the finish of the present series of Not So Much a Programme the BBC intend to discontinue this programme.'

Your decision over this programme did not obviously take into consideration the point of view of the many thousands of viewers who watch and enjoy this programme. It occurs to me that you are catering for the minority, and surely you must realise that this just isn't practical, as the BBC2 Channel are [sic] now proving. I get the impression that the people who ring or write to complain appear to watch the programme solely for this purpose. If these people are offended by this programme, why watch, there is a switch on all Television Sets marked <u>off</u>. Surely they are capable of using it.

Anyone who watched this programme last Friday night when Bernard Levin was criticising Sir Alec Douglas Home would only look on Mr. Levin as an imbecile for saying such stupid and childish things, and in any case the other two gentlemen on the programme made him look so foolish that the only reaction he should have got from this statement was to laugh at him as you would a child instead of taking the poor idiot seriously.

Yours faithfully,
D.J.M.

London SW20
12 April 1965

Dear Mr. Frost,

I was just on the point of giving back my rented Television Set as there is nothing worth viewing now that your programme has come to an end. But reading the papers this morning I saw a gleam of hope seeing that you are having talks about doing another of your shows.

Seeing your programme last night I felt like going to a funeral and felt such an emptiness in not being able to see you and your colleagues on 3 nights a week during the dark days of winter any more.

After all it is us, the viewers, who help to finance the BBC in paying £4 for the licence and I think we should have a say in what we want to see especially when it concerns a programme like yours which is full of talent and life.

I hope you will come back in the very near future because until then my set will be mostly switched off.

Good luck to you and all the members of your cast for the future,

**(Mrs.) R. T. A middle-aged viewer
and
Miss G. T. A young girl in her 20s**
I could add hundreds of names from all walks of life and all ages to our signatures just to let you and the BBC know how much your programme is appreciated.

Edinburgh
12 April 1965

**To: The Director General British Broadcasting
Corporation**
NOTSOMUCHA
Sir,

We, the undersigned, wish to protest against the arbitrary closure of 'Not so much a Programme, More a Way of Life.'

We believe that this programme (and its predecessor TW3) provided entertainment of fine calibre and we are unable to understand why it has been taken off. Satire, after all, is a well established genre. The corpus of English literature without Pope, Swift, Samuel Butler, Shaw, Orwell and Eliot would be emaciated indeed.

Unfortunately, few read satire nowadays and yet it as refreshing and necessary as ever it was. Ned Sherrin's team, in our opinion, ventilated so many avenues of contemporary life that BBC television without them will be so dull as to be almost dead. What a feast for the intellect lies ahead of us on Sunday evenings – A Tale of Two Cities; Evening Service; ancient Hollywood film; Sunday Night at the London Palladium (on the rival channel); and whatever is to be substituted for David Frost's show. Not very stimulating! Has the Sunday evening programme any virtue except that it is free from any taint of satire?

Yours etc.
R. H. and 47 other signatories

CHAPTER TWELVE

THAT WORD

It is perhaps hard to remember now when we have lived through an era that celebrated the clothing manufacturer French Connection's cheeky rebranding of itself as FCUK, that the very slight rearrangement of those four letters almost caused national apoplexy in November 1965. Kenneth Tynan, the former theatre and subsequently film critic of *The Observer*, now the Literary Manager of the National Theatre and no stranger to controversy, deliberately spoke the word aloud on Sherrin's latest version of *TW3*, called *BBC-3* – although as a more accurate reflection of the programme's content, the producer might well have stuck to his original thought of using as the title *It's All Been Done Before*. *BBC-3* was, in truth, a pale imitation of the wit and innovation that had marked *TW3* – with this one exception.

In June 1965 the British Board of Film Censors had banned the film version of John Cleland's eighteenth-century novel *Fanny Hill: or, the Memoirs of a Woman of Pleasure*. In *The Observer*, Tynan launched a fierce diatribe against the decision, claiming that 'erotic stimulation is a minor but perfectly legitimate function of art'. Invited by Sherrin to discuss on television the topic of censorship, Tynan decided to take the attack to the opposition from the kick-off. That accounts for the somewhat convoluted manner in which he manages to get the word he wanted to say into his reply to a question posed by Robert Robinson on what was really a different topic entirely.

The reaction was truly astonishing. The momentous Unilateral Declaration of Independence by Rhodesia which had taken place two days before gave way to this new controversy, which temporarily also wiped the Vietnam War off the front pages. The files in the Written Archive are bulging with the cries of the outraged. There were questions in the House of Commons, condemnations in the press and Mary Whitehouse wrote to the Queen. (The Queen forwarded the letter to the Postmaster General, Anthony Wedgwood Benn, who said that he didn't think it was his job to interfere with the BBC.) In public, Mrs Whitehouse contented herself with the observation that 'Mr Tynan should have his bottom smacked'. Presumably she was unaware of the fact that Mr Tynan was a dedicated and proselytising bottom-smacker himself and, indeed, it appears from his diaries that when he wasn't at the National Theatre or writing his column for *The Observer*, he spent most of his time spanking the bottom of any woman whom he could persuade to allow him to do so.

There were four motions set down in the House, supported by 133 Labour and Tory backbenchers, attacking both Tynan and the BBC. Tynan had not warned either Sherrin or Robinson that he was going to use the word, but their protestations to that effect were not always believed, such was the intensity of the furore. The BBC came out with an official statement that was essentially a fudge – neither condemning nor approving what had been said but rather expressing regret for the offence that had been taken. Huw Wheldon, the Controller of Programmes, on the other hand, openly stated his support for Tynan, telling the press that he found the subject had been handled 'responsibly, intelligently and reasonably'. Such public approval for Tynan's dastardly action merely stimulated the letter writers to new heights of anger and reinforced their belief that the BBC was taking the country to hell in a handcart.

It seems logical that this section should begin with a transcript of what was actually spoken in the BBC studio at Television Centre on Saturday 13th November 1965, the night that a single word stampeded the country into a national fury.

TRANSCRIPTION OF A DISCUSSION CHAIRED BY ROBERT ROBINSON ON *BBC-3*, 13 NOVEMBER 1965

CLAPPING

CHAIR: Mary McCarthy [is] the author of several novels and the best-known perhaps is *The Group*. Kenneth Tynan is the Literary Manager of the National Theatre. Tomorrow night Kenneth Tynan is to propose at a forum at the Royal Court Theatre that censorship in the theatre should be abolished and on this, Mary McCarthy is agreed. Both feel that censorship in any form is illegitimate. Now I wonder if this means, Kenneth Tynan, that you'd allow a play to be put on at the National Theatre in which, for instance, sexual intercourse took place on stage.

TYNAN: Oh I think so, certainly. I mean I doubt if there are very few rational people in this world to whom the word 'fuck' is particularly diabolical or revolting or totally forbidden. I think that anything that can be printed or said can also be seen, and I don't see why we should draw a distinguishing sort of division between great art, which is allowed to do these things – D.H. Lawrence and so forth – and the fourth-rate striptease show. I think the important thing is to allow all artists, however base and however great, to express themselves. Now if in doing that they contravene the laws of libel or obscenity in this country then they must answer in court, but I don't think they should be censored before they do it. I think they should be allowed to do it, say it and show it and then after that, the authorities, the Director of Public Prosecutions can, after that, decide whether action should be taken, but not before it happens.

Isle of Aran

14 November 1965

Sir,

Four-letter words are neither entertaining nor educational. I PROTEST – vehemently.

Yours etc.,

L. F. (Mrs.)

Smethwick

17 November 1965

Sir,

I have tried to calm down since Saturday night after seeing B.B.C.3 – I was so angry I couldn't write – everyone who had anything to do with that programme should be dismissed immediately.

If Mr Kenneth Tynan wants to talk as he did – why not keep it till he gets home and talk to the people he works with if they can stomach him – we do not want any more programmes like Saturday's performance in our own sitting rooms and as we pay £5 a year I reckon we can say what we want.

Has anyone at the B.B.C. got any teenage children??? Do we want the next generation thinking of nothing but Sex? Does using bad language do any good? You have lost a few more viewers through Saturday night's bit of work.

My weekend was ruined and if this R[obert] R[obinson] and K[enneth] T[ynan] receive all the curses I have wished upon them then they certainly will suffer.

If I had lived near to the B.B.C. I would have waited for Mr T to tell him what I thought of him. If he can't do any good in this world it would be far better for him to keep away from Television and Radio for ever.

N. W.

P.S. I am still seething even after writing this – K.T. must go and everyone like him – let them have their talks in their own homes – not ours!

University of Essex Union
14 November 1965

Dear Sir,

We the undersigned wish to express our deepest disgust and contempt of the incident in last Saturday's 'BBC3' programme in which Kenneth Tynan outraged public decency on television by uttering a four letter obscenity. The general approach to life personified in BBC programmes is manifestly trite, vulgar, unentertaining [sic] and unedifying. We suggest the BBC break its commitment to a policy of moral anarchy, of being vulgar and 'iconoclastic' for no worthier motive than puerile desire to shock its public, and renew its commitment to the edification and entertainment of the public. It should at least portray the decency and responsibility to avoid lowering its viewers to its own wretched and worthless level.

The BBC should restrict its time to those communicators who are acting from noble motives, if the word still has meaning amid the indifference and irresponsibility thrust down our unwilling throats. If it is incapable of fulfilling this task, the service should cease to demoralise the nation by closing down.

As a token of the BBC's acceptance of its responsibility to the public, we request that Mr. Tynan be publicly and permanently banned from further appearances on television.

Yours Sincerely
Eight names

The students at Essex University were obviously of a different character from the extreme left-wing activists I met there in the early 1970s!

Swansea
14 November 1965
To: Lord Normanbrooke, Chairman, B.B.C. London W1
Sir,

Last night, in the privacy of my sitting room, and to my family [?sic] a man, employed by your Corporation, uttered, through the medium of a Television Broadcast known as 'B.B.C.3' a foul obscenity which has never before been heard in my home and, I trust, never will be heard again. I refer to the use of the word 'fuck' spoken before my wife, my teenage daughter, my teenage son, my son's teenage girl-friend and before me. *[No mention of the dog, I notice.]*

Great breaches of taste have occurred all too frequently in the past and have been 'glossed over' by an apology in the press. It appears that no effective measures are being taken to prevent recurrences of such behaviour.

I therefore require by return of post a <u>personal</u> apology from yourself and the producer of BBC3 and from the moron who uttered the word and also details of what disciplinary action are being taken in relation to this episode.

Failing some adequate and immediate assurance on this point I intend instructing my lawyers forthwith to issue an injunction against your Corporation in the Chancery division to restrain you from repeating such insulting behaviour.

Yours truly,

F.S.W.

Oxted Surrey

17 November 1965

Sir,

Once again, you have outraged the public, by allowing one of your smutty-minded liberals to use a word, in his mindless argument, which is considered obscene in law, and for which people can be prosecuted for its use in public.

How do you think we are to instil decent standards and morals into our young people, when you allow all this destructive <u>filth</u> to get by on the B.B.C. programmes?

Your producer, Ned Sherrin, has given great offence to the public before, with his TW3 shows, and it is more than time he was removed – you to [sic].

My teen-agers have been taught all their lives that certain words are obscene, yet so-called educated and responsible men allow filthy words and dirty ideas of morals to pass their lips on our screens very frequently.

The once great B.B.C. is becoming like a tenth rate revue, with smutty, filthy talk, quite unchecked.

It is also a forum for all extreme Left-wingers and coloured England haters. Either you, or they – preferably both – must go.

R. T.

Bardsey, Nr. Leeds
16 November 1965

To: Sir Hugh Carleton Greene, Director General, B.B.C. London W1

Dear Sir,

I regularly watch B.B.C.3 and it is a programme I thoroughly enjoy. On Saturday last during a discussion on Censorship of the Theatre etc., a man called Tynan used a four letter word. I am amazed by the fact that a man can use such a word on Television, which goes into millions of homes, without fear of the consequences, but if the same word is used in the street in the presence of a Police Officer then that person is taken to Court and charged with using obscene language.

I have spoken to a number of men who saw this programme and they are agreed that this was a most offensive remark and they were all grateful that their wives and children were not present.

One opinion being freely expressed is that there is far too much of this pornographic material coming from Television Sets and the interesting thing is that it is invariably from B.B.C. It is apparent that you and your colleagues are completely out of touch with the public.

I suggest that you have the power in your hands to do a great deal of good but with the above item, and plays such as 'Up the

Junction', you are helping to lower the moral standards of the community.

    Yours faithfully,

    T.E.W.

              Dover

       19 November 1965

To: Daily Mail cc. Brigadier Clarke MP; the B.B.C.

    <u>That word</u>

    I have just read your article in today's Mail. As a Ranker Officer, in that I reached my Colonelcy the <u>hard</u> way, the statement that the present uproar comes from the Grundies is utter balls; knowing the vocabulary of the Barrack-room, all the four-letter words are familiar, and <u>you</u> are obviously confusing the BBC's responsibility to it's [sic] <u>employers</u> – the Public – with censorship.

    Radio and T.V. are just as much Public Services as the Gas Board or the Water Board. If instead of gas they piped H2S, or instead of water they piped stinking sewage into our homes, we should at once do something about it; so must it be with Radio, T.V. Theatre &c.

    I realise you have to write a load of old codswallop for a living, but spare us the indoctrination and stop telling us that the B.B.C. is an independent body responsible to no-one; they are responsible to US, the apathetic, Moronic and long-suffering Public.

    You may have heard of me, since the Mail made much of my having discarded my war decorations over the Beatles MBE together with world-wide reaction in Press and Radio, cabled congratulations reaching me from as far apart as New York and Capetown &c.

    Stop 'kidding' your readers that objection to sewage means censorship, and if you don't like outspoken comment, apply that word to yourself!

    Yours sincerely,

    F.W.W.

London N13
16 November 1965

Dear Sirs,

Further to the rather childish furore over Mr. Tynan and
BBC3, my wife and I (who both saw the programme) would
like to say that we fully support Mr. Tynan in this matter and
completely agree with him that 'the word' was used quite
correctly and neutrally, as a perfectly valid – and indeed the best
possible – illustration to a serious point in a – presumably – adult
discussion on a very serious matter, viz. Theatre Censorship.

We would urge you to ignore the present fuss and allow the
whole matter to die a natural death.

Yours faithfully,

K. H.

Telegram from Altrincham, Cheshire sent to Harold Wilson,
House of Commons, London SW1
17 November 1965

APPALLED BEYOND DESCRIPTION WITH BBC PROGRAMME
LAST SATURDAY AND URGE STRONGEST ACTION AGAINST
THOSE RESPONSIBLE STOP APOLOGY MADE BY BBC
COMPLETELY INADEQUATE

Romford, Essex
25 November 1965

To: BBC Programme Planners

Wake up BBC and clean up our screens, or this family will
have to get rid of its TV set when our children are old enough to
join us for evening viewing.

Whatever Kenneth Tynan and his fellow 'intellectuals' may
think, his expression means something very sordid to most
people in this country – it lost its ancient meaning years ago.

I don't belong to any organised pressure group, I am just
a young mother trying to bring up my children in a Christian

home. Let these so-called intellectuals keep their permissiveness and low moral standards, but let them be much quieter about it, and let the vast majority of people in this country carry on trying to lead decent normal lives and bringing up their children to do the same, unhindered by this tiny, but far too noisy minority.

Yours faithfully,

C. J. (Mrs.)

London SW10

15 November 1965

To: British Broadcasting Corporation, Langham Place, London W1

B.B.C.3 13th November 1965

Dear Sirs,

Knowing full well the virulence and energies of reactionaries among the British public, as opposed to the lazy middle-of-the-road type like myself, I feel sure that you will have been inundated with letters in the majority condemning Kenneth Tynan's use of 'the Word'.

I do not take a stand on the moral issue of whether the 'word' is to be used or not. I am indifferent to its use. All I know is that it is a word used frequently in the English language by all classes of society from schoolboys to old men. I have reservations as to whether or not it is used by women as a whole, but some do use it in certain contexts.

Nobody wants the media or the arts to be solely a projection of swear words, but I can see that the use of the 'Word' in certain contexts would be ideal for a playwright.

This is the point that Tynan was trying to make and I feel he should not be slandered by misinformed and misguided people when they take what he says out of context. There is as well, the matter of British hypocrisy which comes into play with a word like this.

Yours sincerely,

D.B.J.

Eastbourne, Sussex
14 November 1965

To: The Director General, The B.B.C., London

Dear Sir,

This is the first letter of protest I have written to you as I am not given to rushing into print. In company, however, with a great many others (from whom you have no doubt heard by now) I find it no longer possible to keep silent over such episodes as occurred on BBC 3 last night. The deliberate use of obscenity and the statement by Mr. Kenneth Tynan that he could see no objection to sexual intercourse being depicted on the Stage is one more step in what appears to be your Department's attempt to thrust decadence down the public throat.

This is a great disservice to the Country by a wonderful medium which could in fact, if it so chose, be a source of strength and of stiffening to the present rotting fibre.

I also wish to protest against yesterday's unkind mimicry of Her Majesty the Queen. She is in no position to answer back and her whole attitude is one of <u>service to her people</u>.

Can the same be said of your attitude?

Yours truly,

R.H.L.

London SE3
18 November 1968

To: Sir Hugh Greene, Director General, BBC, London

Dear Sir,

I write to tell you that Mr Tynan did not offend me, nor, so far as I can discover, any of my friends when he said fuck on T.V.

A pity the BBC felt compelled to apologise.

Yours faithfully,

W. R.

Bishop's Stortford, Herts.

15 November 1965

To: Director General B.B.C. London W1

Dear Sir,

Out of a sense of social responsibility and because of my revulsion at the failure of your staff to observe normal standards of decency in speech, I am writing to say that I and my wife both support the widespread attacks made on you for the abysmally wretched example of vocabulary recently used in 'B.B.C.3'.

Over and over again your corporation declines to accept responsibility for moral leadership [with its] apparent readiness to thrust cruder and cruder language into our homes. Please do not reply to the effect that we 'can always turn it off'. This is an argument that evades the issue. The damage is often done before one could reach the switch. It certainly was the case last weekend. And please do not think that I cannot 'take it'. I had five and a half years as a private infantry soldier including 15 months in a P.O.W. camp and know all the words; but I do not subject my family and friends to such language in my home.

Your corporation has reached an incredibly low level and has defiantly done this in the face of decent opinion for years. It is a great shame on you, Sir, that you and your senior staff are so pusillanimous and devoid of either intellectual or moral perspicacity in this matter of standards in speech and drama. We have had a bellyful of filth, violence and smut.

When will you see that these are not letters from cranks and 'fuddy duddies' but the expressions of people who are not prudes, but people with a normal sense of the standards of decency which bring respect to the real character of this country?

Yours with tarnished respect,

W.J.G.W.

Glasgow
15 November 1965

To: Controller, B.B.C. London

Dear Sir,

The work of the schools is being undermined by certain B.B.C. programmes.

In particular I refer to the Saturday night programme – B.B.C. 3 – in which Kenneth Tynan made an obscene remark.

In addition the remark nausiated [sic] me. It was the first time such a work [sic] had been heard spoken in my house.

It is essential that you take action in this matter by sacking all those responsible.

Yours faithfully,

J. McC.
Headmaster

Swansea
15 November 1965

To: Lord Normanbrooke, Chairman, B.B.C., London W1

Dear Sir,

What is happening to this decent Country of ours that the very air should be sullied by such filthy remarks as used by Mr Tynan on Saturday? It was just sheer luck that the younger members of my family were not listening.

I see from the Press that the Producer Ned Sherrin said, 'It was not arranged beforehand'. This shows slackness at some level and if it continues the younger generation will soon be deprived from 'viewing' at all. Obscenity isn't the sign of an advanced mind, it is on the contrary – decadence.

The old phrase 'There is something rotten in the state of Denmark' is all too applicable to us today. There is certainly something rotten in the state of England and the sooner we deal with it, the better.

Yours faithfully,

D.M.S.

Horsham, Sussex

15 November 1965

To: Lord Normanbrooke, Chairman, B.B.C. London W1

Dear Sir,

When in the name of God will you rise up and say the B.B.C. will be used to build a Britain clean and strong and free? If you don't fight, it will all be farmyard in two years time.

Saturday's B.B.C. 3 was a disgrace to you and Britain.

Yours truly,

L.M.

Woodford Green, Essex

15 November 1965

To: Sir Hugh Carleton Greene, B.B.C. London

Sir,

I have never had occasion to write to you before, in fact I had hoped that it would be unnecessary on this occasion for before writing this letter I have been waiting for some official expression of regret regarding the obscene performance of Kenneth Tynan on B.B.C.3 on Saturday 13th November 1965, but it appears that you, and the Corporation by it's [sic] silence, entirely agree with the obscenity perpetrated. Many viewers, of which I am one, have in the past endured the almost constant flow of bad language in the vain hope that the B.B.C. would grow up but it seems that if one doesn't complain the filth will get worse.

I would remind you that the four letter word used by Tynan if used in the street to the annoyance of any person would lead to his arrest, having regard to this I would be obliged to know exactly what action you contemplate, if Tynan is not to be prosecuted I would like to know why not?

In conclusion as you are a State employee I intend to take this matter up with my Member of Parliament for it appears to me that your directions in the matter of programme content leave very much to be desired.

Yours disgustedly,

J. S.

Renfrewshire
16 November 1965

To: The Controller of Programmes, BBC, London

Dear Sir,

It was with regret that I read in my morning paper the apology issued by the BBC for Mr. Tynan's choice of vocabulary in last Saturday's 'B.B.C.3' programme.

The discussion was, as you admit, a serious one and it should be difficult to discuss anything involving emotional and moral opinion without offending someone!

My own reaction was, I hope, not unique. The immediate reflex was: 'Gosh, he's been and gone and done it now – what a chump!' but this was followed by a realisation that to develop the argument with the, at times, almost painful sincerity that Mr Tynan displayed, he had chosen the best possible word for the context. He forced me, at least, to realise perhaps more sharply than anyone before what is involved in rejecting censorship. Protest from the expectedly monotonous quarters was to be expected; what is disappointing is to find these pressure groups obtaining the comfort of an official apology.

Yours truly,

G. T.

M.A. (Oxon.)

Farnham, Surrey
15 November 1965

Dear Mr. Wheldon,

I have just been reading in my newspaper the report on 'that word' used by Mr. Kenneth Tynan in the BBC3 programme on Saturday night.

I am very glad that Mr. Robert Robinson who comperes the show says, 'I didn't expect such a word. I don't think Mr. Tynan should have used it'. I was watching with my son aged seventeen and that is exactly my feeling. I did NOT like that word being used.

When I see the remark attributed to you in this morning's newspaper I feel I must protest. You are reported as saying, 'It was quite germane to the subject'. I don't see what that has to do with the use of this particular word. Mr. Tynan could have used another word which would have expressed his meaning quite adequately.

What might be acceptable amongst men on their own is not, under any circumstances, acceptable amongst mixed company. Would your wife, or your mother, allow this word to be used in her company with young people present?

I am very disappointed that you did not come right out and say that it was an unpleasant word, and that you were sorry it had been used.

Yours sincerely,
Mrs. B.M.G.

Wigan, Lancs.
19 November 1965

Dear Sir,

I have already written to my M.P. to protest constant attacks on Christian morality and decency.

The cause of my complaint was the recent use of a word – the filthiest in the vocabulary of human swine, which seems only to have stirred a ripple in official B.B.C. quarters. I am a veteran of the First World War and used to rough company but never have I heard the word used in such a shameless, barefaced way.

I consider it Your Duty, as a monopolistic corporation, to maintain a high standard on television and to protect the public from a crew of evil men who admit to no standards of right and wrong.

Yours faithfully,
J. G.

London W5
Sunday

Dear Huw Wheldon,

As a family man of 51 and a past president of a Chamber of Commerce with no pretence of being prudish and easily shocked, I was dismayed and disgusted to listen to Kenneth Tynan and Mary McCarthy using television to give themselves notoriety by using words which they knew would cause indignation and disgust.

There is little excuse as Robert Robinson was equally to blame for putting the question. It would certainly seem to me that the 3 people concerned need more censorship, certainly not less. If your comment is correct as reported in the Sunday Express I can only say that you too should be dismayed and certainly appalled!!

If you think it was a reasonable discussion I can only say that the majority of viewers will consider you 'out of tune' with their ideas of the type of people that should be allowed to televise [be on television?]

I am writing to the minister concerned, also to my M.P. to air my views.

Yours in disgust

T.E.G.

P.S. The next suggestion would be that Homosexuals would be allowed to perform their act on the stage without censorship!

We can only assume that by 'their act' he didn't mean a rather cheery rendition of the song 'YMCA'.

Rotherham, Yorkshire
15 November 1965

To: The Director General BBC

Dear Sir,

My wife and I wish to protest in the most vehement terms about certain pornographic language used in 'BBC3' on Saturday evening. This took place in a discussion on censorship!!

Please censor your 'so called' unscripted programmes to ensure that the barrack room doesn't encroach into our sitting rooms <u>with</u> or <u>without</u> giving us due warning. We can switch off only after the event if not warned. We have no desire to be 'modern' or 'with-it' if this is what is entailed.

Has the BBC gone completely SEX mad? Please grow up, BBC.

Bitterly disappointed, I am, Sir,

Yours sincerely,

J.G.G.

Purley, Surrey

15 November 1965

Dear Mr. Wheldon,

I see from the newspapers you are receiving protests about Mr. Tynan's language on Saturday night.

I hope you will pay no attention to these. The word was used in the course of a serious discussion and I see no reason why the adult section of the population should be expected to live at the mental level of children.

I do not understand why some people watch an outspoken programme and then at the end of it protest. Instead of licking their lips they could switch off.

Yours truly,

R.G. R-H.

London SW1

15 November 1965

Dear Sirs,

I protest that without my knowledge or consent unacceptable language is brought into my home.

As the notepaper indicates I am in the entertainment industry and quite familiar with dirt. I transferred to record the tapes of 'the trial of Lady Chatterley' for Pye, a recording which <u>featured</u> the four letter word. I also handled the 'Rugby Songs' before and after the filth which existed from beginning to end was bleeped out. It is, however, a matter of indifference to me who buys these records. If people decide to play them in their homes that is their affair. But to allow this sort of stuff to be broadcast indiscriminately is deplorable.

'Network of the Nation' it used to be – why not drop all pretence and call yourselves 'Network of the Gutter'?

Yours faithfully,

J.R.H.

Leicester

15 November 1965

To: B.B.C. London

Dear Sirs,

I must write to say how utterly disgusted we were with the programme on Saturday evening.

Whilst I think Mr. Tynan's language is absolutely revolting why was he asked such a question in the first place? Whatever is happening to England, when a family sit during an evening for entertainment that's the filth that is handed out?

Most of the plays seem to bring a bedroom scene which I think is most unnessary [sic] and also most embarrassing with a teenage family.

Best of luck to Mary Whitehouse.

Yours faithfully,

B.E.H. (Mrs.)

Whitstable, Kent

15 November 1965

To: Sir Hugh Carleton Green [sic] B.B.C., London

Dear Sir Hugh,

Although the four letter word used by Mr. Tynan is not particularly edifying, and when used commonly suggests a limited vocabulary, I would far rather listen to Mr. Tynan – four letter words and all – than to the aggravating sounds that come

forth from people like [*Sunday Telegraph* journalist] Peregrine
Worsthorne and [novelist] Tom Stacey!! Can they not be replaced?

Sincerely,

Mrs. J. G. H.

Eastbourne, Sussex

15 November 1965

**To: The Director General BBC Broadcasting House,
London**

Sir,

I wish to vigorously protest about the filthy expression used in
the BBC3 last Saturday night. My family, and my son's family were
aghast and completely embarrassed. Do you pay people to proceed
with the disgusting work of breaking down decency and dignity?

I have served in the crew of an oil tanker and a front line
private soldier so am qualified to discuss this sort of off colour
programme, which seems to be getting more and more frequent
on BBC programmes.

In my judgement someone should be made to pay for this
breach of trust as I regard it.

Yours truly,

J.W.A. L-W

Bradford

20 November 1965

**To: The Director General, B.B.C., Broadcasting House,
London W1**

Dear Sir,

I wish to protest most strongly about the use of a four-letter
word by Tynan on TV last week.

Someone on the executive of the BBC must have known that
Tynan was a 'risk' and yet he was allowed on the programme.

I think that you have lost control. In my view, you ought to
resign now.

A drive must be made to 'clean-up' T.V. and all kinky literary and theatrical types kept off the air.

If any more four-letter words and obscenities are spewed-up into my home again, via the T.V. screen or Radio, I shall do everything I can to persuade my MP and others to have you dismissed from your post in the event of your failure to resign.

Yours very seriously,

T. L.

Middlesex
14 November 1965

Dear Mr Wheldon,

After seeing you on Television many times, I formed the opinion that you were a decent, honourable and fair minded intellectual. After reading your comment on last night['s] discussion with Kenneth Tynan and Mary McCarthy, I now put you in the same class as the other sex mad intellectuals who infest and seem to control the B.B.C.

I hope you have a copy of Lady Chatterley's Lover in your office or home, to refresh your memory, in case you have forgotten what this four letter word looks like in print.

To let this stuff come into peoples [sic] home via Television, is absolutely revolting. You don't need one censor at B.B.C. you need a dozen to stop this, and plays like Up The Junction. I nearly always look at B.B.C. to escape the stupid advertising on I.T.V., but after this latest filth offering, I feel like suffering the advertising to escape another outrage.

Yours faithfully,

A.C.L.

Wimbourne, Dorset
14 November 1965

Dear Sir,

Travelling in a bus on Saturday the language of two lads of about 14, forced me to administer a light cuff to the ear and the words, 'Watch your language, you're on public transport'. The reply 'so what?' was not unexpected, but my form of censorship was successful, and the four letter words ceased. I am unable to do the same to my television set when I am treated unexpectedly with the same word by a supposedly better educated man than myself. The types of lads I spoke to are just the sort who return from an evening pounding the streets and gaze at the screen and are relieved to think it is now the done thing to use such words. It is not long ago the use of the word Bloody was taboo on B.B.C. now hardly a play is complete without one or two. How long before other words are to become commonplace? Judging by the stupid nonsense talked by your freedom loving character on B.B.C.3 it won't be long before we shall enjoy a programme of sexual intercourse in all positions I presume.

Heaven knows I am not a prude nor even an ardent church goer, but surely the medium of television is debased by the lapses from good taste. If this is adult viewing then for heavens sake let us not condemn our teenagers. As a parent I find it difficult enough to guide my two youngsters without this rubbish coming up at unexpected moments. I think it's time there was censorship for B.B.C. Television programmes and last week's B.B.C.3 wouldn't have got even an X certificate.

Yours sincerely,

J. L.

Leicester
14th November 1965

Sir,

I wish to record extreme disgust at Saturday night's edition of BBC 3. The item about sexual intercourse on stage and subsequent use of an obscene word is completely beyond all bounds of taste and I cannot find any justification or excuse for the inclusion of such material in <u>any</u> programme, much less one intended for general viewing.

If you incline to the view that the 'Chatterley' case has rendered such words respectable I contend that they are nevertheless obscene and would rightly render anyone using them in the streets liable to prosecution.   In any case surely no one wishes to pretend that they like these words to come into everyday conversational usage. I regret that I can impose no penal sanction upon you to support my view.

Certainly not Yours,

J. Orton

*J. Orton from Leicester? Surely this couldn't be the author of **Loot** and **What the Butler Saw**, born and raised in Leicester, in one of his prankster moods, could it?*

London N10

16 November 1965

To: Director of B.B.C.

Dear Sir,

You have my sincere sympathy over the ridiculous publicity given to the use of the word 'Fuck' in a serious discussion which gave no offence at all. If he had said 'That four lettered word' we should have all known what he meant but I presume no fuss would have been made! Is this not sheer hypocrisy?

Yours faithfully

F.M.

Married with 2 children of 22 years and 15 years

Southampton

15 November 1965

To: The Director General, B.B.C. Broadcasting House London W1

Dear Sir,

B.B.C.3 – Television

I have never written to the B.B.C. before but I feel that perhaps one should write in this case from I hope the 'other side' in the four letter word episode on last Saturday's B.B.C.3. I only hope that the B.B.C. will not take too much notice of all the old women of both sexes and all ages (to quote the Bishop of Southwark in another context) who object to a serious discussion and the perfectly natural use of a simple word. If infants or innocents stay up to listen and are shocked surely it will not do them any harm. The normal adult should be able at 11 p.m. to listen to a reasonable discussion and the use of a word in its proper place without the usual display of hysterics.

An adult approach is something too seldom seen on Television let us have more of it. Let the old women have their 'Sooty' by all means but do not deprive the rest of us of adult programmes.

My only complaint is that there is too much infantile rubbish shown and the adult programmes are getting fewer and fewer, even 'Tonight' has gone which used to be a glimmer of hope in the dullest of T.V. nights.

Yours faithfully,
R.J. Nicoll

The above letter was read by a beleaguered BBC Secretariat official who passed it on to someone else to reply to it. Scrawled across the top was the relieved request 'A nice word to this friend, please'

Co. Wicklow, Ireland
16 November 1965
To: The Information Department B.B.C. London W1
Dear Sir,

I am a regular listener and viewer of your programmes, but unfortunately, I have recently been prevented from enjoying them by a bout of influenza that held me bedridden.

It thus came about that I missed last Saturday's programme in which, so I am informed, Mr. Tynan uttered his celebrated four-letter word.

An awful lot has since been written and said on the subject, but I alas remain completely in the dark. I still don't know <u>what</u> the word was.

Would you please enlighten me?

Yours sincerely,

Dr. A.J. P.

Please note that the B.B.C. did not succumb to the temptation to write back with two words, the first being the word in question, the second being 'off'.

CHAPTER THIRTEEN

TONIGHT AND MAN ALIVE

These two programmes were staples of the BBC schedules from the first appearance of *Tonight* in February 1957 till the last appearance of *Man Alive* in 1981.

Tonight was the current affairs magazine programme which was transmitted each weekday evening between 6 p.m. and 7 p.m., initially filling the gap left by the Toddlers' Truce, the time when parents could persuade children upstairs to bed by telling them that television had finished for the day. ITV, when it started, took advantage of the BBC's temporary disappearance to grab the audience and hang on to them for the rest of the night.

Tonight boasted an array of talent from the urbane, unflappable main presenter Cliff Michelmore to other featured presenters who included Derek Hart, Fyfe Robertson, Julian Pettifer, Chris Brasher, Polly Elwes, Brian Redhead and the peripatetic Alan Whicker. Behind the camera were young directors like Jack Gold and Ned Sherrin. The executives included the future Director General Alasdair Milne and the future Controller of BBC1, Donald Baverstock. Because it was live it could respond to breaking news, as it did most famously on 22 November 1963 when the viewers of *Tonight* became almost the first British people to learn of the assassination of President Kennedy.

Tonight was fast, fresh and amusing, an enormous contrast to the stately pace at which BBC television had traditionally moved. The programme's success advanced the careers of most of its staff and the result was an exercise in empire-building which included *The Great War*, an outstanding 26-part series about the 1914–1918 war which was timed to coincide with the fiftieth anniversary of its outbreak. The essence of *Tonight* was its ability to mix the light-hearted with the serious, best evidenced by the topical calypsos sung by Cy Grant, the first black actor to appear regularly on British television, with words frequently written by Bernard Levin. When Sherrin moved from *Tonight* to originate *TW3*, he took with him many of the elements that had made *Tonight* such a success, including the idea of the calypsos now sung by Lance Percival.

Man Alive was the umbrella title for the series of innovative individual documentaries which were edited by Desmond Wilcox. If *Tonight* was essentially a light-hearted series with occasional moments of seriousness, *Man Alive* produced essentially serious documentaries with occasional moments of levity. Shortly after the series began, the born-again Christian Malcolm Muggeridge made a film about the Playboy Club called *Lift Up Your Skirt*, a clear reference to the morning radio slot *Lift Up Your Hearts*.

Sex was only one of the subjects that *Man Alive* attempted to cover that would appeal to the audience as being innovative, but it frequently did so in a sensational manner which reflected the fact that Wilcox had worked for the *Daily Mirror* before moving into television. He knew that sex, class and religion were subjects that fascinated most people but that, although television had mostly steered clear of such topics, those such as the satire programmes that had approached them had frequently made their producers and performers if not rich, then at least famous. Wilcox hired programme makers who gave the *Man Alive* strand class, while never forgetting that his job was the acquisition of ratings. He made a winning success of it. The film which perhaps was the strand's greatest triumph was *Gale is Dead*, the story of 19-year-old Gale Parsons, who died a drug addict on 11 February 1970 during the making of the film. She had been brought up in no fewer than 14 institutions and was convinced that she mattered to no one.

Both *Man Alive* and *Tonight* poked their cameras into places where none had gone before but of course such intrusion came at a price – as the BBC's correspondents were quick to point out.

The Royal Scots Greys, Catterick Camp, Yorkshire

27 June 1958

To: Sir Ian Jacob, KBE, CB., British Broadcasting Corporation, LONDON

Dear Sir,

I refer to last Monday's Television programme entitled 'Tonight', in which a Darlington factory girl named Pat Brennan was interviewed by Cliff Michelmore on her meeting with the Duke of Kent at my regiment's All Ranks Dance. Miss Brennan claimed to have danced with Prince Edward and to have taught him to 'jive'.

On arrival at the dance, Prince Edward was accosted by three young women who opened the conversation by asking for his autograph. His Royal Highness, as a host, offered the girls a drink and out of courtesy danced once with Miss Brennan. That was the end of the incident except that all three girls subsequently proved rather difficult to shake off. [T]hese girls had been commissioned to get a story by some disreputable newspaper reporters who were lurking outside the dance-hall and who had naturally been refused admission.

Prince Edward and incidentally my regiment repeatedly suffer from the attentions of gossip-writing journalists whose puerile tittle-tattle invariably has a defamatory slant. The damage done by this sort of unwelcome gossip is less when it is confined to those newspapers which are known for their sensationalism and lack of integrity: it is far greater when such gossip is publicised by an authoritative organisation like the British Broadcasting Corporation. The programme to which I refer was in my opinion indiscreet, in poor taste and showed complete lack of consideration and respect for a member of the Royal Family.

Yours sincerely

A.W.D.

Nuneaton

22 October 1957

To: Sir Ian Jacob, K.B.E., C.B., The Director-General, B.B.C., Broadcasting House, LONDON W1

Dear Sir,

Television Broadcast about Nuneaton in 'Tonight' 14th October

As you may be aware, such strong exception has been taken, both here in Nuneaton and throughout the country, to this broadcast that His Worship the Mayor, Councillor R. Wilkinson, convened a special meeting of the Borough Council and it was unanimously decided to ask you to receive a deputation led by the Mayor.

It has, no doubt, been reported to you that the Mayor protested vigorously to Mr. Geoffrey Johnson Smith when he called upon him the day after the original broadcast and you will have had the opportunity of gauging the extent of the local feeling from the second programme which, it was understood, was arranged to portray Nuneaton's reaction. For your further information, I enclose some of the local newspapers in which reference to the programme was made. I assume you have seen the report of the Council Meeting in 'The Times' this morning. I enclose a copy of the report and I have a complete recording of the meeting last night which can be available.

I hope, Sir, that these papers will give you some idea of the widespread indignation and the very real feeling of resentment that exists here and I hope you will feel able to receive His Worship the Mayor and his deputation. The monthly meeting of the Council will be held on Wednesday of next week so that if you could ask your secretary to telephone me regarding an appointment before then it would be much appreciated.

Yours faithfully,

A.A.C.

Nuneaton

13 November 1957

To: Mrs. G. Windham [Wyndham] Goldie [Head of BBC News & Current Affairs] Lime Grove Television Studios, London W1

Dear Mrs. Windham Goldie,

On return to Nuneaton last evening, I reported upon the conversations we had during luncheon yesterday to the Committee which has been appointed by the Council to deal with Sir Ian's offer to send cameras here again with the object of presenting another portrayal of the town.

I reported that you had agreed to give us roughly 10 minutes on 'Tonight' and that we had agreed that the programme might contain extracts from [the first] film. So far as this suggestion was concerned, the Committee was not prepared to acquiesce at all. They still feel that the film as originally shown and the commentary were not only bad taste but deliberately defamatory and most objectionable and on no account do they wish any further extracts from it to be shown again.

They have, therefore, instructed me to prepare for their approval a general idea of the theme to be followed and I shall be writing to you again about this. In the meantime, I should be pleased to hear from you as to when you think this programme might be produced.

I also mentioned that you had invited me to be present at the editing of the film and the commentary and the Committee were most insistent that I should accept this offer.

Kind regards,

Yours sincerely,

A. A. C.

Town Clerk

Mayor's Parlour, Town Hall, Blackpool

29 January 1962

To: H. Carleton Greene Esq. O.B.E. Director General, THE BRITISH BROADCASTING CORPORATION, London W1

Dear Mr. Carleton Greene,

'TONIGHT' – Thursday 25th January 1962

Consequent upon the number of complaints received and the very strong feelings of resentment engendered I write to register the strongest possible protest against the content of the Alan Whicker contribution in the TONIGHT programme on Thursday last.

It is considered that the programme was guilty of a serious and calculated slander upon that conscientious and hard working body of people comprising the proprietors of the Blackpool boarding houses.

The burden of the complaints is:- that the programme allowed several persons to describe 'Blackpool landladies', collectively and without reservation, as 'robbers' and to utter every other insult imaginable; that improper language was used; that the programme seemed intent upon reviving an outdated music hall joke at the expense of the proprietors of hotels and boarding houses; that it is remarkable in the extreme that Alan Whicker was able to find assembled in one room so many with such unhappy memories of Blackpool landladies without there being present a single person with an opposite experience.

I cannot recall any other matter which has aroused such strong feelings of resentment and injustice among the residents of Blackpool. I shall be grateful to hear if you have any proposals to offer by way of reparation and if you can please supply me with the name and address of the Club in which the interviews were conducted and the names and addresses of the persons interviewed.

Yours faithfully,

(Alderman) C.C. J.P.

Mayor

Mayor's Parlour, Town Hall, Blackpool

10 February 1962

To: H. Carleton Greene Esq. O.B.E. Director General,
THE BRITISH BROADCASTING CORPORATION,
Broadcasting House, Portland Place, London W1

Dear Mr. Carleton Greene,

'TONIGHT' – Thursday 25th January 1962

I thank you for your letter dated 7th February which reached me only this morning.

I am sorry to tell you that I cannot find your letter a satisfactory reply to the criticisms and complaints which I outlined to you and I know it will not pacify the many who continue to smart under the affront of the programme. Accordingly I must consider what further steps I may take. Meantime, I shall be grateful if as requested in my earlier letter you will be good enough to supply me with the name and address of the Club in which the interviews were filmed and the names and addresses of the persons who were interviewed.

I was very surprised to read in your letter that my letter to you had been published in the press. Many requests for a copy of my communication were received but these were refused. Inevitably there were many press references to the letter but I have no knowledge of the letter itself being published. Can you please let me know in which newspaper the letter was published?

Yours sincerely,

C. C.

Mayor

Mayor's Parlour, Town Hall, Blackpool

22 February 1962

To: H. Carleton Greene Esq. O.B.E. Director General,
THE BRITISH BROADCASTING CORPORATION,
Broadcasting House, Portland Place, London W1

Dear Mr. Carleton Greene,

'TONIGHT' – Thursday 25th January 1962

I refer to my letter dated 10th February and would be pleased to receive a reply to the queries posted in the letter.

Much of the heat engendered has passed but there are still a number whose concern remains and I am anxious to resolve this matter as soon as possible. Accordingly, I look forward to the courtesy of your early reply.

Yours sincerely

C. C.

Mayor

Mayor's Parlour, Town Hall, Blackpool

2 March 1962

To: H. Carleton Greene Esq. O.B.E. Director General, THE BRITISH BROADCASTING CORPORATION, Broadcasting House, Portland Place, London W1

Dear Mr. Carleton Greene,

'TONIGHT' – Thursday 25th January 1962

I acknowledge the letter dated 27th February under the signature of your Chief Assistant which replies to my letter dated 10th February.

It is disappointing to find that you decline to furnish the information requested and particularly when I realise that approximately one month has elapsed since I first expressed myself to you on this matter.

I cannot escape the feeling that in view of the very close and, I think, friendly relations which have existed between our two Corporations from the days of the earliest outside broadcasts my representations upon a matter which seemed by its lack of balance and fairness to jeopardise the livelihood of so many might have been received in a more co-operative and productive way. However, there does not now seem any point in pursuing the matter and I will close our correspondence by expressing the hope that our first complaint to the B.B.C. will prove to be the last.

Yours sincerely,

C. C.

Mayor

Goldsmiths' Hall, Foster Lane, London EC2
31 October 1961

To: H. Carleton Greene Esq. OBE,
BBC Portland Place, W1

Dear Mr. Greene,

I am a great admirer of the B.B.C. but I cannot stand the treatment 'Tonight' gives us. All I beg of you is that it learns some administrative manners. Otherwise people like myself will really give preferential treatment to I.T.V., whose various organs still, thank goodness, think it natural to take trouble over their performers.

In April I brought back some jewels from Lisbon, was told 'Tonight' would like to see them, took them to the studio, was told they were no good for TV, was then kept waiting two hours in an uncomfortable hall, until the promised car arrived. No apologies, no explanations.

Last week 'Tonight' asked for seven jewels to be sent to the studio, sent a Ford car with a non-uniformed driver with a chit of paper purporting to establish his suitability to take this £100,000 load. We refused. Eventually two security men turned up; we sent two silversmiths and the jewels arrived too late for the programme. No explanations, no apologies either then or later. I enclose our account for the half day which the two skilled men gave to 'Tonight'.

All I want to record is indignation that the power which 'Tonight' has so cleverly built for itself should allow the programme to behave like arrogant barbarians.

With all good wishes,

G. H.

Domestic Refrigeration Development Committee, London W1
12 January 1962

To: The Director General British Broadcasting
Corporation, Broadcasting House, Portland Place
London W1

Dear Sir,

The members of my Committee which comprises the leading manufacturers in the domestic refrigeration industry in this country – I attach a list – are most disturbed at the strong bias shown in the programme on discount trading which took place in 'Tonight' on Wednesday January 3rd. Although I saw this programme at the time, I have waited until obtaining a transcript before writing to you.

The domestic refrigeration industry attaches great importance to the maintenance of prices and regard this as of value and benefit to the public. They are quite ready and, indeed, anxious to explain the reasons for their views. It does not seem at all right that the BBC with its highly authoritative position should allow a programme to come down so heavily on one side and to arrange the programme so that in fact no other outcome could reasonably be expected. I hope there can soon be another programme on this subject. This Committee would be very glad to provide an effective exponent of price maintenance.

I shall look forward to hearing from you on this in order that I can report as soon as possible to my Committee.

Yours faithfully

C. C.

The Medical Protection Society, London W1

19 November 1962

To: the Director General, B.B.C. Broadcasting House W1

Dear Sir,

Programme 'Tonight' on 6th November 1962

At a recent meeting of the Council of this Society, attention was drawn to an interview between Mr. Kenneth Allsop and Dr. Byrne which was included in the programme 'Tonight', broadcast in the London area at 6.50pm on the 6th November 1962.

The main result of the broadcast interview was clearly to draw attention to the occurrence of errors in surgical operations causing injury to patients, with particular reference to operations performed upon the wrong patient or on the wrong side, limb or digit of a patient. The whole tone and content of the interview appeared to imply that errors were frequent. In fact, they are extremely rare.

The impression was created that surgeons and their teams are unreasonably careless in the precautions taken to avoid such mishaps. The impression left with the viewer was that it was common for a patient to have the wrong finger amputated and for several swabs to be left in the body of a patient. It is extremely unlikely that any such mishap will occur. The result of this item was to undermine the confidence of the public in the medical and nursing professions and to cause anxiety to those viewers who were themselves or had relatives about to undergo surgical treatment.

The Council hope that the Corporation will recognise the damaging effect on morale which this kind of programme can produce.

Yours faithfully,
A. F.

Northern Ireland Tourist Board, Royal Avenue, Belfast
14 November 1959

To: Sir Ian Jacob K.B.E. British Broadcasting Corporation, Broadcasting House, London W1

Dear Sir Ian,

Last Friday the 9th, in the 'To Night' programme there was a feature about Belfast given by Mr. Alan Whicker which has caused the very greatest resentment here. In my capacity as Chairman of the Northern Ireland Tourist Board I and my colleagues felt the programme to have been most damaging to Northern Ireland.

Only one side of the story was given. Great stress was laid on the fact that our Police carried revolvers however it was because of the activities of the IRA. The public houses are open from 10am to 10pm. A comparison should have been made with other countries. It was remarked that during the last war conscription did not apply here. No mention was made of the large numbers that joined the Forces. Great emphasis was made that Betting Shops were filled with unemployed persons but the number of employed due to new factories is greater now than it has ever been. The last point I would make is with regard to some of the photography. Pictures of City Hall, Stormont, etc. appear to have been taken on a foggy day.

Mr. Alan Whicker had a tremendous amount of information at his disposal from the BBC, the Government of Northern Ireland and the Tourist Board that he ignored completely.

The Controller of Northern Ireland Broadcasting has made a public apology on the local T.V. news programme but the least that can be done is that an apology is made on the National Programme.

Yours sincerely

H.J.W.

South African Embassy, Trafalgar Square, London WC2

19 November 1963

To: Mr. H. Carleton Green, Director General, BBC, London W1

Sir,

I must lodge a protest against the gross partiality displayed against South Africa in the programme 'Tonight' on 18th November 1963, when, against photographs of violence and squalor in South Africa, glowing extracts from articles that had appeared that morning in The Daily Express were read in an attempt to discredit both South Africa and The Express.

To judge from details of dress in some of the pictures, several must have been taken up to 30 years ago; and yet the B.B.C. allowed itself to present them as depicting South Africa today.

I would be the last to claim that squalor and violence do not occur in South Africa, as indeed they occur in every country where there are disparate peoples with different levels of development living side by side. But to present this as the daily face of South Africa is not only superficial but it gives offence to truth as well.

Differences of opinion on whether our policy of parallelism is the final solution to our political problems may be honestly held. But until our critics advance a workable alternative, mere facile sneers and jibes are hardly the weapons that become a serious organisation such as the B.B.C.

Yours faithfully,

M. C. L.

Paxton Road, Chiswick, London W4
17 November 1966

To: The Controller of Programmes, B.B.C.2 Television, TV Centre, Wood Lane, W12

Dear Sir,

I watched with much displeasure your 'Man Alive' programme last night entitled 'A Roof Over Your Head – Part 4. Try Buying It'. I am myself a member of the Estate Profession and am sick to death of continually seeing it pulled to pieces by B.B.C. Television. There are good and bad in all professions and it's about time the B.B.C. realised that there are good Estate Agents.

Perhaps you are not aware that there are four main Professional Bodies whose members have to abide by a code of conduct and this code has been drawn up to protect the public. The only person who ever seems to have his say on these programmes is Mr Roy Brookes who is not a qualified Estate Agent but started his career as an Advertising Agent. He has made his name purely from his advertisements in the Sunday papers and not on his professional merit.

The entire programme gave the impression that all Estate Agents are rogues without any suggestion whatsoever that reliable firms were to be found. I would suggest that next time you are arranging a programme on this subject you contact one of the recognised Bodies for advice before slandering the entire profession.

Yours faithfully,

D.A.F.

St. Benedict's Hospital, London SW17

4 August 1967

To: D. Attenborough, Governor B.B.C.2. (TV) Kensington House, Richmond Way, London W14

Dear Mr. Attenborough,

'Man Alive' Programme August 2nd 1967 Life Sentence I –
Pamela

I am sorry to say that I have a very serious complaint to make to you about a statement made in the introduction to this programme. 'The beginning of another day in St. Benedict's Hospital, Tooting; a geriatric hospital where the old are sent to die and sometimes the young to live'.

The statement is completely untrue and gives an utterly false and misleading impression of the hospital to the general public. It also falsely implies that Pamela La Fane's plight is far worse than it actually is. This is NOT a hospital for the dying. This is a geriatric hospital i.e. a hospital for the diagnosis, and medical treatment of anyone of pensionable age. [Presenter] Jeremy James may not realise the dreadful damage he has done to my work to help the elderly. The simple people believe what they [see] in black and white and will in future be [too] frightened to come into St. Benedict's (their relatives will have the same unfounded feelings) and I shall have great difficulty in persuading them to come in for treatment and reassuring them that they are not going to die. Jeremy James may not realise that he may have undone the hard work of many years by doctors, nurses, physiotherapists, occupational therapists and medical social workers.

Secondly, I wish to complain most seriously that the name of the hospital was spoken on the programme without the producer having asked permission. Had we been asked we should certainly not have granted it since it had nothing to do with the programme. I was deeply shocked and I consider Mr. James to be a most irresponsible young man.

Yours sincerely,

J.S.W. M.D. M.R.C.P.

Sutton Coldfield
28 February 1968

**To: Mr David Attenborough Director of BBC2,
Broadcasting House, London**

Dear Sir,

Re Programme MAN ALIVE, Tuesday 27 February – 9.5pm.

Too often, unfortunately, whenever programmes concerning immigrants in this country are produced the majority of spokesmen seem to be uneducated persons. This has the effect of creating the impression that the immigrant groups have only uneducated people within them.

The behaviour of Mr. Egbune and the rubbish uttered by Frankie X do nothing for the course [cause?] of racial relations or for the respect of the none-white [sic] immigrants in this country.

In the future it would be of greater benefit for the promotion of harmonious relationships if more intelligent – even if forthright and dogmatic – persons would be invited to appear. I feel that Tuesday night's programme did nothing but caused disgust and contempt both to the immigrants and to the hosts of this country.

Yours faithfully

C. R.

United Daughters of the Confederacy, Lexington, Kentucky
1 April 1968

**To: The Honorable Managing Director, British
Broadcasting Corporation, Broadcasting House, London,
England**

Dear Sir,

Some very disturbing and dissappointing [sic] reports have been received from contacts in the British Isles and gleaned from reviews in the Radio Times and the Daily Telegraph of the program entitled 'Daughters of America' on the MAN ALIVE hour.

Apparently the information gathered in the United States by the team led by Mr Adam Clapham, Director, Features and

Science Programmes during September and October of last year has not been used in the manner which we were led to believe it was being assembled.

Mr Clapham called at our business office and headquarters building in Richmond, Virginia, and indicated that the United Daughters of the Confederacy was chosen because they wished to have a patriotic organization represented in their review of women's work in this country and that we had been selected because the United Daughters of the Confederacy had no political overtones concerning itself only with the cultural side of life.

Reports from the British press and personal reports from England to me indicate that in your broadcast the United Daughters of the Confederacy were more or less ridiculed, and maligned; and the broadcast, instead of emphasising the cultural contributions of the UDC really downgraded the fine contributions they have made during their entire history. The broadcast fails to point out the patriotism of the United Daughters of the Confederacy.

Particularly do I deplore the fact that your commentator, Mr Desmond Wilcox, chose to focus his lens on one of our older members who was totally unaccustomed to television interviewing and completely nonplussed. This was a most ungentlemanly and discourteous act and a total violation of the privileges granted the team. They had been advised time and time again that I, as President General, was to be interviewed and quoted.

Because of the failure of your organisation to use the material collected through the generosity of the United Daughters of the Confederacy for the furtherance of cultural activities among the English women and because of the manner in which it has been used, this is to ask that the film be withdrawn from your library and destroyed.

This letter is being written with the approval of our legal advisors.

Yours very truly

A.N.H.

CHAPTER FOURTEEN

GRANGE HILL

Grange Hill provoked more correspondence than any other programme on children's television. It did so because it portrayed school life more realistically than anything that had been seen on television to date.

The first popular school series was *Billy Bunter of Greyfriars School* which ran from 1952 until 1961 and was adapted from the stories written by Frank Richards and which had started to appear in the boys' comic *The Magnet* some years before the outbreak of World War I. Girls' school stories by Angela Brazil sold well as books but in those chauvinistic days obviously not well enough to be adapted for television. The popular Enid Blyton *St. Clare's* books only appeared as a bizarre Japanese anime series in which the characters sounded as if they were voiced by Americans trying to speak with English accents. There were occasional adaptations of classic stories like *Tom Brown's Schooldays*, and Jimmy Edwards was a popular cane-wielding headmaster in the Frank Muir and Denis Norden sitcom *Whack-O!*, but all these school stories were set in public schools, far removed from the experience of most of the children who watched television. It wasn't just that there was a hole in the market which *Grange Hill* filled. It was that life in a comprehensive school had not previously been considered suitable material for children's television.

The instinctive horrified reaction to the series indicates why it took Phil Redmond so long to sell his concept for *Grange Hill*, which had acquired rejections from every company between 1975 and 1977 before Anna Home at the BBC finally took the plunge. She proved to be an outstanding Executive Producer, championing the series in the face of hostile criticism. The series showed as a matter of routine the petty thefts, bullying, skiving off lessons, vandalism and smoking which the children would have known all about but their parents would have preferred not to have seen portrayed as a fact of daily school life. However, as the following selection of letters makes clear, the series was much admired by adults as well as children who recognised it immediately as an honest reflection of their lives.

Grange Hill ran for thirty years from 1978 to 2008, but its major impact was felt in its first few series. The parents who wrote in to complain were usually middle-class mothers who did not wish their children to be 'infected' by *Grange Hill*, although the very real distress felt by women who thought menstruation not a fit topic for children's television came from all social classes. As we have seen in other chapters, by and large people who write in want to complain. Not many admirers of a television show take the time and trouble to express their appreciation in this way unless it is something remarkable like the Royal Family film. The fact that *Grange Hill* lasted for as long as it did is a tribute to its enduring relevance.

Sleaford, Lincs.
Tuesday 12 February 1980

Dear Ms. Home,

Your 'Grange Hill' series has a devoted following, age range 11–18 plus some staff 35–62 (me) and each episode has allowed us to explore touchy subjects without rancor. [sic] In one episode a caring staff went on Instant Strike and that left children to get into trouble. We found ourselves – my class and I – discussing divided loyalties and responsibilities. The episode involving the insensitive and ill-informed handling of a non-reader sparked off another discussion about the fallibility of teachers – in a defused, impersonal way. The unreasonable expectations of parents could be debated, because Grange Hill allowed this, without disloyalty to pupils' own parents. Because these topics arose naturally out of our normal morning chatter – 'Did you see that bit in 'Mash' where ... ' we can laugh and argue on equal terms – no teacher – pupil – deference – discipline overtones, and we are never in danger of forgetting that 'Grange Hill' is <u>entertainment</u> not Social Studies/Humanities/Religious Studies.

I've taught in Secondary Moderns, private prep, ESN unit, grammar schools – state and Church – for the last forty years, and television, not only children's drama, has been one of my most powerful allies.

I do hope you aren't too badly bruised by criticism of Grange Hill. For every one silly teacher there are a hundred sensible pupils (and me)!

Yours sincerely,

Mrs. J. B.

The National Association of Head Teachers

5 March 1980

**To: Managing Director, B.B.C. Television,
Television Centre, Wood Lane, London W12**

Dear Sir,

'Grange Hill'

I have received a complaint from one of my members about an incident when a false fire alarm was caused by a pupil who broke the glass in one of the alarm switches. Another comprehensive school in the same town also had a false fire alarm.

There is no doubt in my member's mind that the incident was brought about by an idea gained from the previous evening's episode of 'Grange Hill'.

It seems to me that the producers of Grange Hill have no idea of the effect that their programme can have on impressionable minds, nor do they realise just how much disruption can be caused by pupils emulating incidents in the television series.

Yours faithfully,

D.M.H.

Sheringham, Norfolk
10 March 1980

To: The Controller of Programmes,
B.B.C. TV, London

Dear Sir,

On Thursday February 28th we had, in this school, our first ever malicious fire call.

I am disturbed that this followed so closely on a similar event being shown on 'Grange Hill' and feel that, whilst the connection would be difficult to prove, it is even more difficult to dismiss it as a coincidence.

Yours faithfully,

P.W.D.
Headmaster

St. Albans, Herts.
5 January 1981

Dear Anna Home,

I am writing to express my disapproval of last Friday's episode of 'Grange Hill'. I objected specifically to

1) the attitudes towards authority and to physical violence in the incidents with the caretaker

2) the language and attitudes of some of the boys towards the girls which fosters the male chauvinism that thinking members of society are trying to discourage

3) the attitude towards promise-keeping and social obligation by the girl on the protest committee

4) the general attitude expressed by the tone in which the line 'they treat us like children' was said and the context.

I can only comment on that particular episode as I do not generally watch the programme, but I have discussed it with other parents and with a teacher in a large comprehensive school who have all expressed doubts about various attitudes portrayed in the series. Reluctantly I have decided to stop my children, aged 8 and 10, from watching. I have never censored their viewing of children's programmes before, but I feel that for their age group 'Grange Hill' is potentially harmful. The virtues of the programme, its 'realism' and avoidance of moral viewpoint, make it popular but also subtly undermining of values I would prefer to maintain.

Yours sincerely,

S. C.

P.S. I expect your reaction will be the inevitable British one involving class. If you do not want to portray middle class values (and I suspect 'Grange Hill' is devised as a counterweight to the charge that the BBC does this) you should consider the dangers of reinforcing middle class prejudices which are just as divisive of society as the opposite.

Seven Kings, Essex

6 January 1981

To: Anna Home
[Executive Producer, *Grange Hill*]

I feel I must write about the program [sic], GRANGE HILL I saw this evening 6th Jan. I am a broad minded adult. I was disgusted to hear girls discussing what happens to them monthly, with boys, surely it isn't necessary. Also Boys discussing about there [sic] Mothers monthly.

I am glad my Son was not here, or any Male, I feel this is very personal to Women, and not to be shouted about on television. It just went on and on about the same thing.

I am very angry about it, and I think it was not fit for any one to watch.

Mrs. L. L.

Wollaton, Nottingham
6 January 1981

Dear Sirs,

Re: Grange Hill – Televised 6–1-81

I wish to register a complaint regarding the content matter in the Grange Hill programme televised at 5.10pm today. I was utterly shocked and disgusted that at a peak viewing time – supposedly children's programmes – I should hear women's monthly periods being discussed by school children.

I know this particular programme has been the subject of complaint in the past, I should have thought therefore you would have been more careful in what you put on the air.

Yours faithfully,

S. W.

Wirral, Merseyside
6 January 1981

Dear Sir,

How much more tasteless can the present series of 'Grange Hill' become?

Can young children look forward to a school girl pregnancy or a discussion on V.D.?

I object to this level of programme

Yours sincerely

D. M. H.

London SW10
9 January 1981

Dear Miss Home,

This isn't simply a fan letter; I've been a theatre critic now for nearly 20 years and this is a critical suggestion.

I was caught by GRANGE HILL almost as soon as it began because it was what I saw when I was waiting for the news. I've continued to see it whenever I can, and have been interested to see individual kids growing up, notably the admirable Todd Carty.

It now seems to me that something might be done to follow their careers after they leave school – not for sentimental reasons, but because life for school-leavers is particularly difficult at the moment and it would be both interesting and helpful if a series could be devised showing how they cope with it.

You may think that five p.m. would be the wrong time for such a series, but I believe young people who follow the fairly sophisticated stories that GRANGE HILL copes with are likely to care a bit about what is going to happen to them when they leave school and are quite possibly unemployed.

If you think this is a dotty idea, just take my letter as routine fan-mail for a programme I admire very much.

Yours sincerely,

B.A. Young
Theatre Critic, Financial Times

Wythall, Birmingham
Wed 12 Jan 1981

Dear Sir,

I am surprised and annoyed that the B.B.C. continue to screen 'Grange Hill'. The content and quality of the programme leave much to be desired and this only serves to undermine the hard work done by schools throughout the country.

To illustrate acts of thieving, bullying, smoking and other stupidities for young minds is to promote them – they become accepted behaviour. No doubt the writer attempts to include a moral to his story but these are so often completely lost to young minds incapable of abstract concepts.

As Head of Lower School in a comprehensive it is part of my responsibility to recommend reading, watching and listening to children and parents. Until there is a radical change I shall do everything in my power to discourage the watching of this particular B.B.C. production. This is sad because in many other aspects the B.B.C. does a superb job assisting in the educational process.

Yours faithfully,

C.W. E.

Eastleigh, Hants.

Dear BBC,

I am writing to complain about the disgusting children's programme 'Grange Hill'. I must say most of it is either untrue or exaggerated enormously. I have just finished watching the fourth episode on the 9th of January, I have never seen anything so stupid as teachers actually punching one another, it's just a load of rubbish and I don't think it should be shown on television.

I know there are a lot of people who would agree with me and who would like to have the programme taken off the television.

Yours sincerely,

C. A. (Miss)

Beverley, N. Humberside

26 January 1981

To: Executive Producer, Grange Hill, BBC TV, London

Dear Ms Home,

The most recent edition of the 'Radio Times' features an article on 'Grange Hill' in which the following appears ... 'hardly any of the protests come from children who enjoyed 'Grange Hill' in their millions.'

I enclose the letters written by several of my pupils about the current series. The letters followed a lot of lively discussion and were part of a classroom exercise but contain their opinion not mine. They would be delighted to hear from you in some way and appreciate that you may not have the time to answer individual points.

I think it is interesting that some of them think the Grange Hill regime is too liberal. In rural East Yorkshire we are, so far, free from the declining standards of behaviour in London schools as depicted in 'Grange Hill' (i.e. some pupils do write on toilet walls but so far nobody has wrecked the toilets). However I and many of my colleagues are concerned that in depicting a view of school life, 'Grange Hill' may be responsible for encouraging the acceptance of that view as normal and to be copied.

I hope you will find time to acknowledge the pupils' efforts.

Yours sincerely,

T. B.

English Department

Molescroft, Beverley

20 January 1981

To: The Producer, BBC, Grange Hill, London

Dear Ms [Anna] Home,

I thought you would be interested in my opinions of 'Grange Hill'. My criticisms in lessons, you always see them in the corridors, and you hardly ever see them in the playground. The vandalism in the new series is a bit imagenary [sic] and to [sic] much for the children to have done. Also Tucker is not as naughty as he used to be, and all the other children too. My praises are that it is a quite true to life programme and that all the children do cheek the teachers and smoke, and change signs round ect. And if the programme was on a bit longer, and didn't end in such exciting places it would be even better!

Yours sincerely,

H. G.

Beverley, N. Humberside

20 January 1981

To: The Producer, BBC, Grange Hill, London

Dear Ms. Home,

I thought you might be interested in my opinions of Grange Hill.

<u>Criticisms</u>. My criticisms on grange hill are the punishment there never seems to be much punishment. It could of been Something Very Important and all they get is a telling off I don't think its enough they all get away with it to [sic] easily another thing the teachers at grange hill seem to be very soft with the children I wish I had teachers like that but I still enjoy the programme it is very enjoyable.

Yours sincerely,

S. M.

P.S. ask Tucker if he is well

Beverley, N. Humberside

20 January 1981

To: The producer, BBC, Grange Hill, London

Dear Ms. Home,

I thought you would be interested in my opinion of 'Grange Hill'! I think it is rubbish. I turn off the T.V. went [sic] it is on and then turn it back on to watch PADDINGTON. I think the new series is good but there is a lot of villains. The teachers are not strict enough.

Yours sincerely,

C. P.

Beverley, N. Humberside

20 January 1981

To: The Producer, BBC, Grange Hill, London

Dear Ms. Home,

I thought you would be interested in my opinions of 'Grange Hill'. When it first came on I thought it was very good. But now it is nothing like a school because they don't have a uniform and they don't have enough punishment in it and it is getting to be a load of rubbish.

Yours sincerely,

J. W.

Northampton
28 January 1981

To: BBC T.V. Children's Programmes

Dear Sirs,

I have previously written to you on the vexed subject of Grange Hill. I can now say I find the new series equally obnoxious as before but because of my dislike I watch extra carefully in order to be fair to all concerned.

I do not doubt that in some areas school[s] are run and children act in such a manner as those portrayed, but I cannot understand why, if you must glorify the worst aspects you cannot also show some of the good points as well. Aren't there any?

My own two daughters are not now so very young but there must be many children watching at that time of evening who are puzzled and bewildered at some of the subjects discussed e.g. menstruation. Also I do not see why I should have to listen to ill-mannered boys shouting their desire for a pee all over my living room.

Yesterday's episode however irritated me more because Doyle was seen sitting in class reading a girlie magazine. The naked bum of the young lady on the cover was clear to all and I felt that to be a gross invasion of my house and standards, especially as newsagents now do not seem to display these magazines so prominently. I shall await your comments, but please don't tell me that I could switch off because that I will not do, being concerned with other children's interests as well as my own.

Yours,

S. M.

Charlbury, Oxon.

Dear Sir,

I was shocked to again see Pogo Patterson playing a major part in the Grange Hill series on BBC TV. Who does this child think he is? In my opinion he has very little acting talent and is fat to the point of obesity – it is definitely not musels! [sic] His physical appearance may not be his fault, but why are fat people portrayed as being so unpleasant?

I am now retired and derive a great deal of pleasure from watching children's television, and so I also know what I am talking about.

A child like the actor who plays Pogo should never have been admitted to drama school, if his acting in Grange Hill is the best he can do. If this is a typical product of today's drama schools, then I dread to think what the future holds for British drama.

May I add that I think Grange Hill is an excellent series, and some of the other actors and actresses are superb. Why does Pogo Patterson have to mar an otherwise enjoyable programme?

Yours faithfully,

G. S.

Liverpool
10 February 1987

Dear Sir or Madam,

On behalf of the students of this unit I have been asked to formally lodge a complaint concerning the disgraceful innuendo aimed at school guidance units, in your 'Grange Hill' programme of Friday 6th inst.

The head teacher, Mrs McCluskey implied that units such as ours were for mentally disturbed pupils. We believe she said something like 'Girls not right in the head would have to go to the special unit'. Taken across the country nothing could be further from the truth.

May we inform your stupid scriptwriter that most units in this country are set up for a special type of pupils. Not dickheads as [s]he implies. They are for pupils who, for the time being, are unable to cope with, or adapt to the normal demands of secondary school. Pupils like us who seem to fail in the sphere of personal relationships especially with unsympathetic teachers who lack sensitivity and compassion and who always seem to get their own way.

So do us a favour and lay off giving our type of unit a bad name. Unfortunately so many of our secondary school friends watch your programme and jump to unreasoning conclusions.

Yours faithfully,

S. J.

Birmingham

23 October 1987

Dear Sir/Madam,

I am a student on a CPVE course at Garretts Green College. I am writing to say how I felt really upset when Grange Hill was on BBC1 in the episode when Samo and Faye were studying in the Sixth Form common room. Somebody mentioned about the CPVE and did it in a way that implied it was a course for thick people. Whoever mentioned [that] was wrong.

I also did not like when Stephen had said that they are THICKO'S because they were on that course. He is wrong. There is somebody who also is on the course who had got 3 'O' levels and 4 CSE's, so we can't be that thick.

Thank you for making time in reading my letter.

Yours sincerely,

C. P.

Newtown, Co. Donegal, Eire

To: Series Coordinator, Grange Hill, B.B.C. TV Center, London W12 England

Dear Sir/Madam,

I would like to commend you on a fabulous television programme. I am a native of New York and I have never seen such a good show. When my family moved to Ireland seven months ago the first show I heard of was GRANGE HILL.

After watching GRANGE HILL a few times I came up with a story idea. It involves an American boy who comes over to England to live with an uncle and goes to GRANGE HILL. The

'YANK' gets into fights regularly about his accent, clothes who's who in American football, and his love of practical jokes. Work schemes are one of his hobbies.

I was also wondering if you could tell me when, if any, auditions are being held in the month of June. I have been in five theatre productions, three of which I starred. In nine-teen-eighty-seven I was in a New York fashion show. I am 5'2', 6 stone and I am 12 years old.

Thank you very much for your time.

Bon Jour,
M. C. Jr.

Gorleston-on-Sea, Norfolk
17 February 1988

Dear Sir,

During an episode of Grange Hill put out on February 16th a 'recruiting poster' for CND is shown several times in as many seconds.

Surely the programme is appalling enough with incipient brainwashing which I thought was against BBC rules anyway.

Yours sincerely,

B. P.

Gorleston-on-Sea, Norfolk
16 November 1988

To: Director General B.B.C. London W1

Dear Mr. Hussey,

Jonathan Aitken M.P. for Thanet and a friend for many years has suggested I write to you over a complaint I made sometime ago about 'Grange Hill'.

In one of the February episodes a large C.N.D. poster was shown several times. I protested that Children's television is no place for incipient C.N.D. propaganda.

The producer of Grange Hill replied that 'after a search of the February episode no trace could be found of the offending shots and that I had mistaken the CND poster for one showing the Grange Hill logo'!

I know a CND poster when I see one but not having access to videos of the period could not take the matter further.

A few days ago I saw the same CND poster again.

No doubt you will wish to look into the matter from the propaganda viewpoint and the BBC's integrity.

I have great affection for the BBC programmes apart from those of a political nature which seem to condemn always the Conservatives who seldom merit even feint [sic] praise.

Sincerely yours,

B. P.

Salisbury, Wilts.

To: Phil Redmond, Elstree Studios, London

Dear Phil,

How are you?

I am writing to you with a problem about drink. I find kids of my age drinking a lot of alcohol and unfortunatly [sic] I am one of them. I almost died twice through excessive drinking and it made me very violent and bad tempered. I started drinking from a very early age and found it hard to come to terms with the fact that I was a Alcoholic. After a lot of courage I decided to attend Alcoholics Anonomous and shortly I will be seeing a psychiatrist.

Well to get to the point I was wondering if it would be a good idea similar to the theme on drugs in Grange Hill to have one of the Grange Hill pupils with a drink problem and the effects it has on his body. The drugs theme did really well and I think a theme about drink would also do really well. I've still got a lot of problems of my own, but would love to help other kids with drink problems before they damage their bodies and perhaps kill themselves.

As I stated earlier in my letter I almost killed myself when I was 13 years old from drink and nearly died not so long ago. I am now 18 yrs of age.

Therefore all I want to do is to help other kids and perhaps through the TV series Grange Hill it could do likewise.

Looking forward to hearing from you.

With love

S. C.

PS Will Imelda still be in G.H.?

Southall, Middlesex

6 July 1988

Dear Directors, Producers and Writers of Grange Hill,

I am writing in to ask you why isn't there any Indian children in the Grange Hill cast? There are lots of Indian children between the ages of 10 to 16, who are great actors and actresses, and would love to be in Grange Hill. I hope to hear from you soon. My address is at the back.

Yours hopefully,

A. B.

P.S I think Grange Hill is Brilliant!

Cardonald, Glasgow

Dear Sir/Madam,

I am writing to give you an idea for your program Grange Hill.

My idea is to get someone who is Scottish or maybe even Glaswegian to play a part because I would like to hear a Scottish accent amongst those London accents.

Maybe you could make him a sort of hero who rids off all school bullies.

I hope this idea comes in handy to your writing career.

I myself would like to be in the T.V. series.

Yours thankfully,

P. M.

CHAPTER FIFTEEN

THE WEATHER FORECAST

'Pray do not talk to me about the weather, Mr Worthing. Whenever people talk to me about the weather, I always feel quite certain that they mean something else.' But, Gwendolyn, the British love their weather. It is the one topic of conversation that strangers of all ages, classes, colours, religions, ethnic origins and sexual orientation can talk to each other about without the slightest fear of social embarrassment. In 1987, when Michael Fish got the weather forecast so badly wrong that he dismissed the very possibility of a hurricane which a few hours later devastated south east England in the worst storm for three hundred years, he was accorded instant cult hero status.

In the days when the following selection of letters was written, the weather forecast was considerably less precise than it is today. Consequently, most forecasts consisted of 'bright periods and scattered showers' and other phrases designed to cover the possibility of most forms of weather – apart, of course, from hurricanes. In David Lodge's novel *Changing Places* set in 1969 the American visiting lecturer Morris Zapp listens to the weather forecast on the BBC for the first time assuming it is some sort of spoof because it predicted 'every possible combination of weather for the next twenty-four hours without actually committing itself to anything specific, not even the existing temperature.'

Michael Kennedy, the well-known journalist and authority on matters of Elgar, Britten, the Halle Orchestra and Lancashire County Cricket Club, once told me of the single most important thing he had learned from his time as the Northern Editor of the *Daily Telegraph*. Recalling his experience with his outraged readers, he uttered the words of someone who had seen the foulest deeds and the darkest depths to which human beings could sink. 'Never,' he said with a shudder, 'never mess around with the weather forecast.' BBC television did it once – now look what happened ...

Boddington Hall, Leicestershire

14 December 1956

To: The Director General, The B.B.C., Broadcasting House,

Sir,

When the Television Authorities decided to discontinue the normal weather charts and forecast during the weekend the decision was no doubt taken with good reason and after careful consideration. But is it realised how dependent on this service a very large section of the community has become?

The television service has done much to educate the public to read the charts. The result of this education is that the charts are missed more than they would have been previously.

It is not only the agricultural community which requires full and accurate forecasts during the weekend. The vast number of people who wish to spend their Sundays in the open air are also affected. For the farmers the Sunday forecast is usually the most important. Should it be possible to reinstate this service it would clearly be an advantage if it could appear at the same time each evening.

I felt it right to draw your attention to this matter before taking it up either in Parliament or by letter to the Press.

I am

Sir,

Your obedient servant,

[Lord] Allerton

House of Lords
24 October 1961

Dear Carleton-Greene,

I write to enquire what are the reasons for the suspension
of the weather forecasts by the various meteorological experts
on Television at 6.18 p.m. and the substitution of a much less
complete forecast[?]

I understand that forecast now takes place at the end of the
programme in its original form. But the hour is late and is not so
suitable for the agricultural community (who are amongst those
most deeply interested) as the previous time of 6.18. Farmers are
mostly early risers and as such are disinclined to sit up until this
late hour.

I would say that I have found the forecasts to be very valuable
and that I regret very much that they are no longer available at
their old time.

Yours sincerely,
[Lord] Allerton

House of Lords
28 November 1961

Dear Carleton-Greene,

You will remember that I wrote to you some weeks ago
with regard to the time at which the weather map is shown on
Television. The enclosed cutting from last week's edition of the
Farmer & Stockbreeder bears out my contention that the present
arrangements are not universally acceptable.

I would be glad if you would let me know whether further
consideration has been given to this matter.

Yours sincerely,
[Lord] Allerton

Taunton, Somerset

21 December 1966

To: The Director of Television, B.B.C. Television Centre, London W1

Dear Sir,

I feel driven to protest against the changes you have recently made to the television weather service. I do this under a number of different hats.

Firstly I would wear the deerstalker of a Geography teacher. For very many years now I have made frequent use of the weather maps shown after the 6 o'clock news. Both for my own personal interest and to increase the interest of the boys whom I teach, I feel that the present map is difficult to comprehend on other than an infantile level.

Secondly, as a Headmaster my Geography and Science staff have expressed their disappointment at the disappearance of a feature which they valued.

Thirdly, as Chairman of a Steering Committee for the Somerset Schools Sailing Association, it is essential for schools to make their own assessments of the weather situation. This is only possible from the information supplied by the up-to-date synoptic charts. The newspapers form a very poor substitute.

Lastly, as a dinghy sailor myself, I have always felt it invaluable to be able to decide from the 6 o'clock weather map whether sailing would be possible the following day or not. The information you provide at 11 o'clock is neither timely nor sufficient. I do hope you will find it possible to review your existing arrangements and give us the weather service we so valued in the past.

Yours faithfully,

R.H.B.

Headmaster

Stevenage, Herts.

20 December 1966

To: Sir Hugh Greene, Director General, B.B.C. Langham Place, LONDON

Dear Sir Hugh,

May I make a plea on behalf of Geography teachers in Secondary Schools that a full weather forecast with meteorological charts be brought back to be shown after the early evening news.

The study of weather conditions commonly prevailing ever the British Isles and the associated charts is an essential part (as it should be) of most Geography courses including those leading H.C.E. 'L' AND 'A' level and C.S.E.

It seems regrettable that in a time of educational enlightenment a public corporation whose programmes are seen in millions of homes throughout the land should seem to be catering for the lowest common denominator.

The rising generation are interested in the subject, and unlike many of previous generations who did not have similar opportunities, do have some understanding of meteorology.

Yours faithfully,

G.L.L.

Geography Master

Vickers-Armstrongs, Barrow-in-Furness, Lancs.

17 November 1966

To: The Director General, B.B.C. LONDON

Dear Sir,

I know that I am not alone in being appalled by the recent changes in weather forecast presentations on the B.B.C.

Before these recent changes this synopsis was of the greatest value to people like myself who require to know not just what the forecasters believe to be going to happen, but also the basic weather facts.

The approach of winter for travellers like myself who regularly cross the Pennines and other areas of high ground, knowledge of the weather situation can be essential to safety. To those of us in the maritime industries such knowledge can also be of great commercial significance, but no doubt you will already have received comments from coastal pilots, port and ship-owning organisations.

My purpose in writing to you is to endeavour to make clear the severe loss which the recent changes have brought to viewers who have regarded in the past the excellence of BBC1's weather programme as a major incentive to switch on. The present mockery of a programme which must be an embarrassment to those conscientious members of the Meteorological service, who have served the BBC's viewers so well, is more likely to persuade us to switch off than switch on.

Yours sincerely

T.V.R.

CHIEF NAVAL ARCHITECT

CHAPTER SIXTEEN

MISCELLANEOUS COMPLAINTS, GRUMBLES, IRRITATIONS, ARGUMENTS, WHINGES AND MOANS

As this final selection of letters indicates, sometimes it must appear to the BBC that not only is it impossible for them to please everyone, it cannot even please anyone. Unless the programme is a gushing tribute to the work of travel agents, estate agents, doctors, dentists, male nurses, the magnificence of Torquay, Skegness, Belfast, Blackpool or Nuneaton and so on it will inevitably attract fierce criticism from those who feel that their profession, town, sport, etc., is being traduced by the manner in which the BBC has covered it – apart from those who are equally outraged that the BBC has signally failed to cover it at all. Certain actors and presenters always induce feelings of violence in a small part of the audience but unless they write to vent their loathing of (1,248 names redacted) we shall never know their identity.

On many occasions I have listened to *Test Match Special*, having told my impatiently waiting female companion that I would join her as soon as I had learned the current score, only to be confronted by the idle witterings of the radio commentators which go on for minutes as they make unfunny remarks about each others' clothes or the irrelevant arrival of a flock of pigeons and do not do what they are paid to do, which is to *tell the audience what the score is*! Now, I had assumed that either this was my individual obsession or that it was the result of the sad loss of the great commentators like John Arlott, Brian Johnston and Christopher Martin-Jenkins and their replacement by commentators of inferior quality. But according to a letter written in the winter of 1946, during the first post-war Ashes tour, it appears that in my intense irritation I speak for many others …

London SW3

26 November 1946

To: The Director of 'Announcers' B.B.C. Portland Place, W1

Dear Sir,

Can you do something before the Test Match starts to protect Cricket lovers against the ignorant complacency and infuriating method of announcing incompletely 'Cricket' news?

Between 7 and 8.30 a.m. a business man can only spend a few idle seconds waiting at the set for flashed news, especially as the general outline is found in his newspaper and to wait 10 mins. idly fidgeting for the time when the special announcement for Cricket leisurely comes through usually causes irritable tensions especially when the announcer rarely follows the first fundamental of sports recording i.e. a bald statement of the scorecard in full.

Could I suggest a short school course for your announcers to be taught the fundamentals of Cricket news and the best teacher would be one of the innumerable school boys who attend Lord's, who assiduously and keenly analyse the result of every ball bowled, sometimes even with diagrams – they would know how to make an intelligent and cogent announcement, with the score card repeated at the beginning and end of the announcement if necessary.

Yours very truly,

C.M.P.

Crowborough, Sussex
9 September 1950

To: BBC Governor Barbara Wootton

Dear Madam,

As a Wireless License Holder I feel I am entitled to write to you – a Governor of the BBC – requesting you to use your influence in connection with that very objectionable item Any Questions. I urge that immediate action should be taken in the following order of priority:-

(1) Terminate this item at once

Failing that

(2) Remove [economist, author and Liberal Party politician] Graham Hutton permanently from this item

Failing that

(3) Confine this item to the West of England Programme, i.e. do not broadcast it in the Home service

I would add that a competent Question Master would not have allowed this feature to have degenerated into the deplorable state it has reached. The audience now come prepared to shriek at the gibes against people who are not able to reply as lustily as the ancient Romans shrieked for the blood of Christian martyrs in the Arena. In the words used by Churchill in 1940 concerning the report of the actions of Leopold of the Belgians – 'it stinks'. It has become an objectionable feature of our public life.

Yours faithfully,

W.E.G.

Crowborough, Sussex

22 September 1950

To: the Director of the Spoken Word, Broadcasting House London W1

Dear Mr Barnes,

You must know as well as I do that whilst many receive this programme [*Any Questions*] as at present presented with acclamation there are as many who are displeased with it. Only on Monday of this week did I hear from listeners in Southampton of their disgust with the particular broadcast of Any Questions which led to my complaint. It does not become a Corporation such as the BBC to tolerate within its programmes controversial matters – unless they also invite to the microphone representatives of the opposite point of view and allow them to there and then refute obnoxious points.

It is beyond dispute that whenever Graham Hutton is included in Any Questions the programme has a Conservative bias. His remarks concerning [Clement Attlee] the Prime Minister in the broadcast which led to my protest were such as should have caused the Question Master [Freddy Grisewood] to have immediately suspended him from the programme. Whether we and Graham Hutton like the Prime Minister or not is beside the point. The fact is that at the moment he is the elected Head of our State and as such should be given the respect due to the holder of that position. The remarks in question were such as one would not use in private conversation let alone in a public broadcast.

I realise that to the mighty BBC this protest is a very minor affair but I still think it worthy of a complete postage stamp and not the half a stamp used on your recent letter which led to my having to pay His Majesty's Postmaster General a postage due fee of 5d, vide attached envelope.

Yours very truly

W.E.G.

A note on the file indicates, thankfully, that five penny stamps were to be included with the reply.

London SW1
14 July 1946

To: The Editor

Dear Sir,

Many people I have spoken to are surprised, as I am, that there was no mention in the 9 o'clock news last night of the result of the cricket match between our two most famous public schools at Lord's.

May I please be given the reason?

Thanking you,

Yours faithfully,

S.S.

English Lake District Hotels Association, Keswick
2 March 1960

To: The Director of Television, c/o B.B.C. Broadcasting House London W1

Dear Sir,

Re: Television Broadcast 'No Passport' 24. 2. 1960

I have to inform you that this broadcast has been discussed by the General Purposes Committee of the above association. I was instructed to inform you, that whilst the Committee appreciate your decision to make a Film of the Lake District, they are very disappointed with the way this film was presented, as it fell far short of the established admiration of the thousands of visitors to Lakeland, from Britain and Overseas, of the beauties and scenery of the district in general, and it was agreed that this was a poor effort, undertaken by two inexperienced youths.

If you wish to obtain some idea of the beauties of the Lake District, and the way in which Films should be taken, I would suggest that you get in touch with the Ribble Motor Services Ltd. Frenchwood Avenue, Preston, Lancs and ask for the loan of their Films of Lakeland. Compare them with the Film which was broadcast on television on 24th February, and I think you will agree my Committee have just cause for complaint.

With reference to the remarks made by Mr R. Dimbleby at
the end of the film, my Committee are of the opinion that these
remarks should be disregarded, as they are unworthy of notice, and
in direct contrast to the established favourable comment of visitors,
regarding the hospitality of the Hoteliers in the Lake District.

Yours faithfully,

R. B.

The British Travel and Holidays Association London SW1

2 February 1959

**To: Kenneth Adam Esq., Controller of Programmes,
B.B.C. Television Centre, Wood lane, London W12**

Dear Kenneth,

I appreciate the number of programmes which have been
broadcast on holiday taking in Britain, but surely we could point
to an extensive list of foreign travel programmes and travel films.

The Association must ask very firmly that British holiday
taking is featured to at least the same extent. 90% of the
population are likely to travel in Britain, whereas little more than
10% are likely to consider travelling abroad.

My committee are particularly concerned with the fact that
the three recent foreign travel programmes were broadcast at the
height of the holiday promotion and booking period. They were
designed in the form of an advertisement, quoting prices, giving
advice etc. In fact I do not believe that the French Tourist office
could have produced a better advertisement, even if they had to
pay the whole of the cost themselves. Had they been shown at
any other time than the present, Spring or Summer for example,
the objection would not be so strong.

The whole picture is getting out of perspective and the public
is being ill-served on obtaining advice about what most of them
want today, i.e. travel in their own country.

Yours sincerely,

J. G. B.

Director General

Torquay Hotels Association, Vaughan Parade, Torquay

30 January 1959

To: The Director of Television Programmes, British Broadcasting Corporation, London W1

Dear Sir,

<u>B.B.C. Television Travel Broadcasts by Richard Dimbleby</u>

There is considerable feeling amongst British resort Authorities, hoteliers and caterers and all concerned with British holidays, in connection with the constant plugging which goes on in favour of holidays abroad. This is not only harmful immediately to those concerned with holidays in Britain but it affects a great number of other trades who are suppliers to British resorts, hoteliers etc. These range in almost every field, from furnishers, brewers, transport concerns and food suppliers etc.

In the past when the question of publicity on the BBC for holidays abroad has been brought up an answer has been received that equivalent publicity is accorded abroad in an effort to persuade foreigners to come over here. We are afraid we cannot accept this explanation. Surely, reciprocal publicity in Brittany and Portugal would only attract a very minute number of foreigners to come over here in comparison with the number of Britishers who must be attracted by the programmes put on, especially under the direction of the well-known personality Richard Dimbleby.

We are sending a copy of this letter to the British Hotels & Restaurants Association and to the British Travel & Holidays Association and to our Member of Parliament.

Yours faithfully,

W.G.S.

Glasgow Celtic F.C., Celtic Park, Glasgow

7 January 1966

To: Andrew Stewart Esq. Controller Scottish BBC, Glasgow

Dear Sir,

We wish to draw your attention to a sports programme which took place on Tuesday night relative to our match against Rangers. In order to put everything into full perspective I wish to give the full details of the history of this programme.

I received a call from the B.B.C. in London. They stated they had been in touch with Glasgow and as Glasgow had a television team at the Park asked if they could have additional photographers on the field. I asked for their assurance that they would not introduce crowd scenes, possible arrests and the like. They would not receive permission unless I had this assurance. This was given to me personally by your representative.

On Tuesday evening matters which did not pertain whatsoever to the match were highlighted in your programme.

1. That the Eire flag flies on top of the Stand.
2. That priests can obtain free admission to Celtic Park.
3. That this match was an orange and Catholic ritual.
4. The battle of the Boyne was mentioned.
5. Mounted police were highlighted.
6. Bottles lying on the ground were given prominence.
7. That the Rangers F.C. had signed on a Catholic and immediately it had come to their notice, gave him a free transfer.

After the match the Chief Constable reported to me that it had been a very well controlled crowd and there had only been four arrests inside the ground where with an attendance of 65,000 it was a very orderly gathering. This programme only took place because we were deliberately misled and told untruths by your representatives. I would ask that they be informed that their presence is no longer welcome.

Yours faithfully,

D. W.

League of Jewish Women London WC1
28 July 1966

**To: Michael Peacock Esq. Director of BBC1 Television,
BBC Television Centre London W12**

Dear Mr. Peacock,

I feel I owe you an apology. When we discussed the World Cup Programme at the Women's Meeting earlier in the month, I felt, at that time, that you were being very anti-feminist in devoting so much television time to football.

In the event you have proved completely right, and I feel I must tell you that my staff (all women) spend the first half hour of every morning discussing the previous day's matches. Tuesday night's semi-final was absolute [sic] compulsive viewing, and I think that there were very few people all over the country who did not applaud the decision you had made with regard to the coverage of this tremendous event. My congratulations to you, not only on your policy but on the way in which the policy has been carried out.

All our hopes and thoughts are with England for Saturday's Final!

With warmest greetings to your colleagues and yourself.

Yours sincerely

Mrs. M. B.

Morriston R.F.C. West Wales
7 July 1962

**To: The Director-General, British Broadcasting
Corporation, London W1**

Dear Sir,

On behalf of my members I must protest most strongly at the utter lack of coverage both sound and television, given by the B.B.C. to the present tour of South Africa by the British Isles Rugby Union Touring Team.

This attitude of indifference by the B.B.C. to rugby is deplorable as whereas we have been inundated in the past month with film of the World Cup, motor racing and tennis, all of which British teams and individuals have not done particularly well, this successful tour of South Africa by a <u>British</u> team is being ignored by you.

You are not loth [sic] to screen the home rugby internationals at the low fee of £2,500 per match, but ignore this major sport on all other occasions and levels.

[Former Wales rugby international and now broadcaster] Cliff Morgan has shown the way with his 'Welsh Sportsview' which in Wales is far more popular than the Dimmock, Jacobs dominated 'Sportsview'.

I would remind you that we are not alone in our thinking on this matter but that this letter reflects the views of all rugby enthusiasts, and indeed all sportsmen, throughout the British Isles.

Yours faithfully,

D. D.

The College of General Practitioners, Bath

28 January 1961

Sir,

May I draw your attention to a programme called 'Epidemic' broadcast on B.B.C. Television on the evening of Thursday, 26th January. The subject was small-pox and whatever medical impression the programme had was poor.

1. The technique of vaccination shown was archaic.
2. Various alleged medical men handled small-pox patients with their bare hands and then used the telephone; put their hands in their pockets etc. without any pretence of washing.
3. One case which was alleged by the 'experts' in the programme to have died of unsuspected small-pox was certified and cremated as a case of pneumonia. This implies a lack of competence – or worse – on the part of at least two doctors – presumably general practitioners.
4. How can anyone detect small-pox infection in samples of jute as the programme perported [sic] to do?

I do not usually watch medical programmes on T.V. They usually give such a false and nauseating picture of medical matters that my stomach revolts. However, I did watch this one and I feel that its obvious defects and its implied slur on doctors call for a protest to the B.B.C.

I have also written to the B.M.A. on this matter.

Yours faithfully,

W.B.S.C.

Cambridge

19 November 1958

Dear Mr Adam,

To belabour the point I was trying to get over to you last night, I do feel, that in view of the great power of Television, very great care should be exercised against maintaining the 'Music Hall' attitude towards dental treatment. Fortunately one programme does do the contrary and is to be congratulated upon it – The Archers.

One feels that people of the intelligence necessary to have control of such a medium must have the intelligence to realise that dentistry is not the absolute painful and all feared procedure that it was, and that this medium should be used to educate the public into a more sane attitude towards the care of their teeth, although this will inevitably produce a greater demand than the profession is, at present, capable of dealing with, there will be a greater chance of some of the public wanting to be dentists.

Yours faithfully,

P.H.F.G.

BBC Lime Grove Studios, London W12

31 May 1962

To: Rex Moorfoot, Esq. Head of Presentation, Room 6043, Television Centre

My dear Rex,

To my great sorrow I was unable to view that admirable programme 'Points of View' last night, but I am told by several people who did see it that, interviewed by Robert Robinson, the Editor of the 'Tailor and Cutter' made reference to the fact that I had been 'pushing' or 'plugging' broad-striped shirts on television. I find it extremely hard to believe, however, that such an assertion could have been made and passed unchallenged, carrying with it an implication that I have received payment for wearing shirts of the kind referred to. This, of course, would be highly defamatory and I wonder, therefore, whether you would be so kind as to let me know exactly what was said.

Yours sincerely,
Derek Hart

AND FINALLY

Coniston, Lancs. [as it then was]
1 November 1962

Dear Mr. [Robert] Robinson,

The son of a friend of mine is again out of a regular job. Would it be possible for you to use your influence on his behalf in getting him a sound, well-paid job with the B.B.C.?

He is not too bright and has no special qualifications, but has a very sociable nature. I am sure he would get on very well with Mr. Dimbleby Jnr., Mr. Cotton Jnr., and Mr. Sylvestor Jnr. Or has influence nothing to do with finding employment with the Corporation and merit alone taken as the criterion?

Yours faithfully,
J.E.G.

APPENDIX

MOST WATCHED TELEVISION IN BRITAIN IN THE 1960S

	Title	Channel	Date	Audience (Millions)
1	The World Cup Final 1966 (England vs. West Germany)	BBC1	30/07/1966	32.30
2	The Royal Family	BBC1/ITV	21/06/1969	30.69
3	Royal Variety Performance 1965	ITV	14/11/1965	24.20
4	News (John F. Kennedy assassination)	BBC/ITV	22/11/1963	24.15
5	Miss World	BBC1	19/11/1967	23.76
6	Apollo 8 Splashdown	BBC1/ITV	27/12/1968	22.55
7	The London Palladium Show	ITV	03/12/1967	21.89
8	Steptoe and Son	BBC	18/02/1964	21.54
9	Coronation Street	ITV	02/12/1964	21.36
10	Mrs Thursday	ITV	22/03/1966	21.01
11	Secombe and Friends	ITV	13/11/1966	20.79
12	Churchill's Funeral Procession	BBC1/ITV	30/01/1965	20.06
13	Howerd's Hour	ITV	12/05/1968	20.02
14	The Grand National	BBC1	30/03/1968	19.86
15	Market in Honey Lane	ITV	03/04/1967	19.47

16	Double Your Money	ITV	08/11/1966	19.47
17	Take Your Pick	ITV	02/12/1966	19.36
18	The Boat Race	BBC1	30/03/1968	19.36
19	Life With Cooper	ITV	16/03/1968	19.25
20	The Morecambe and Wise Show	ITV	12/11/1967	19.14

ACKNOWLEDGEMENTS

I would like to place on record my thanks to James Codd, without whom I would still be trapped in the BBC Written Archives. I would also like to acknowledge the help provided by my Editor at BBC Books, Charlotte Macdonald, Sarah Garnham my publicist and of course my indefatigable agent Luigi Bonomi.